MASTER
YOUR
WINNING
EDGE

Also by Zig Ziglar

Master Successful Personal Habits

Master Your Goals

The Secrets of Successful Selling Habits

MASTER YOUR WINNING EDGE

Zig Ziglar

MEDIA

Published 2021 by Gildan Media LLC
aka G&D Media
www.GandDmedia.com

FIRST EDITION 2021

Front cover design by David Rheinhardt of Pyrographx

Design by Meghan Day Healey of Story Horse, LLC

Library of Congress Cataloging-in-Publication Data is available upon request

ISBN: 978-1-7225-0321-5

10   9   8   7   6   5   4   3   2   1

Contents

Foreword

I n the world of personal development, motivation, and sales, there will never be another Zig Ziglar (1926–2012). His infectious sense of humor, his masterful storytelling skills, his uncanny ability to inspire, and his down-home Southern charm are all part of his legacy. Zig's character was unquestioned. He had a legendary impact in helping people become more, be more, do more, and have more.

In the world of personal development, motivation, and sales, there will never be another Zig Ziglar (1926–2012). His infectious sense of humor, his masterful storytelling skills, his uncanny ability to inspire, and his down-home Southern charm are all part of his legacy. Zig's character was unquestioned. He had a legendary impact in helping people become more, be more, do more, and have more.

What will your legacy be? What lasting imprint do you want to make on the world? With this classic collection of success ideas from Zig Ziglar, you won't leave your legacy to chance. You will be intentional about the impact you make on your loved ones, your friends, and your business associates.

Master Your Winning Edge presents Zig's timeless lessons on success and happiness that have inspired millions of people for more than a generation. This book features his unforgettable lessons about how to get more of the things that money will buy and all of the things that money won't buy. Here's just a sampling of what you'll learn in this volume:

- How winners don't react; they respond.
- Identifying and correcting image problems.
- Steps to a healthy self-image.
- Succeeding in a negative, cat-kicking world.
- Commonsense communication tips for influencing others.
- Creating winning relationships at home and at work.
- And much more.

As Zig grew in his career, he realized this simple truth: if you take all the best skills in the world and put them on the wrong person, it won't do any good. First, you have to develop the person from the inside out. They need to have character and integrity and discipline. They need to be motivated. They need to have a specific goal-setting plan in place so that they can become the right kind of person. Then they have to have relationship skills so that they can work with others. Once you have that person, then you can give them the technical skills, and they can do and achieve just about anything.

That's what this book is about. It's about understanding that skills are critically important, but it doesn't really matter unless the right person is employing those skills.

Once a friend came up to Zig and asked him, "Zig, how come when you speak to a large audience, 80 or 90 percent of your talk is exactly the same talk that you gave the last time?"

Zig just smiled and said, "The truth never changes."

Today things depend more upon truth than ever. We want truth. We want to know that we can count on somebody. We want to deal with people who have honesty and integrity. We want to know that what we stand for and the people we lock arms with have values that line up with truth. As you go through this book and learn these different truths, understand that the more you employ them, the more effective you will be.

A legacy is giving somebody a guideline, a set of rules, a set of beliefs and principles that they can apply to any situation.

Zig's legacy can be summed up in his famous quote, which he often repeats in this volume: "You can have everything in life you want if you'll just help enough other people get what they want."

In our society, people are teaching the ideas of crushing the competition and winning at all costs. But Zig believed that you want to start with having the other person's best interests in mind. When you serve somebody else's best interests first, you build a feeling of trust and endearment. The other person will always remember that. Over time, business will seek you out, because people want to do business with people they know, like, and trust.

As Zig taught, we all go through a journey in life, which he characterized as a process of moving from survival to stability, from stability to success, and from success to significance.

It's not a bad thing to want success, but success is for the most part about the things you can have—money or fame or influence. Significance is helping somebody else be, do, or have more than they thought possible.

Legacy is about significance. When you achieve significance, you achieve the greatest level of joy imaginable, because there is no greater joy than seeing somebody do something they didn't think they could do. That's what drove Zig. And the more we seek significance, the more likely we are to be successful along the way.

It's sometimes said that we no longer live in the information age or the computer age; we live in the connection age. If you're going to live to win, you have to know how to go forward on these foundational principles and truths, which never change despite all the changes that happen before our eyes every day.

Some people say that Zig's ideas are old-school; they don't really apply to today's world. Here's the reality.

Zig said there are absolutes. For example, would you hire an accountant to work for your company who was *relatively* honest? Of course not. That's a truth that never changes. There are relationship principles that never change. People like to be talked to and respected in ways that never change, and these are the core foundational principles that Zig talks about.

So are you going to look to the wisdom of the ages, or are you going to try the new guru on the street? Just remember: there's a reason they call it the wisdom of the ages.

Now more than ever, if you embrace these ideas, you'll stand out. You'll be a rarity. You'll become a leader. You'll become an example. You'll have a competitive advantage, because unfortunately today these principles are not commonly taught. You have to seek them out on your own, and that's what you are doing by reading this book.

ONE

Make Friends
with Yourself

We hear a lot about positive thinking, but positive thinking won't work unless you have a good, solid picture of yourself. In this chapter, I'd like give you some wonderful ideas about how you can build a healthy self-image. You're going to learn how to get along with yourself, which is key to getting along with others. We will look at the causes of a poor self-image, the manifestations of that poor self-image, and, more importantly, what you can do about it. We have to get along with ourselves.

The question I want to start with is, do you respond to life or do you react to it? It's extremely important to know the difference between responding and reacting. The doctors say that responding is positive; reacting is negative. If you get sick and go to the doctor, she'll give you a prescription and say, "See me tomorrow."

You walk in the next day, she shakes her head, and says, "Uh-oh. Your body is reacting to the medicine. We have to change the prescription." But if she smiles and says, "Hey, it's working. Your body is responding to the treatment, and everything is going to be OK," you get excited.

On January 23, 1981, I was in Kansas City, Missouri. It was my final stop in a long week. I'd been doing four-hour seminars north, south, east, and west, border to border, coast to coast, and when I do a four-hour seminar, I expend an incredible amount of energy. On this particular day, we were recording, and when you record, you move it up a notch, because you don't have your body to communicate with. It has to be all voice—inflection and excitement and that sort of thing. So I turned it up a notch. Since I already speak at a rate of about 280 words a minute, with gusts up to about 550, I'd *really* turned it up.

In 1981, recording gear was bulky. One of our boxes weighed over 140 pounds. My son-in-law, Chad Witmeyer, was with me, doing the recording. We had a 3:00 flight back to Dallas. We finished at 1:00. The airlines had said, "You have to be here at least an hour early so we can stow the gear."

The minute I finished, we started assembling all the gear. We packed up as quickly as was humanly possible. We made the mad dash to the airport and got there straight up and down at 2:00. When I walked into the airport, there were two long lines of people. We chose what I thought was the shortest line and prepared to wait.

Almost immediately I noticed that there was a vacant spot down at the counter, with a sign that said, "Position closed." I also noticed there was a lady who was walking around behind the counter. I realized that in a matter of minutes "Position closed" was about to be turned over to "Position open," so I got ready.

Sure enough, the lady walked down, flipped the sign over, looked at the two long lines of people, and said, "Those of you who have seats on the 3:00 flight to Dallas, come over here."

Quick as a flash, I was over there. I got to the new line before anybody else had even left the old line. The lady smiled at me as pleasantly as I've ever been smiled at and said, "The 3:00 flight to Dallas has been canceled."

"Fantastic," I said.

She looked at me strangely and said, "What do you mean fantastic? I just told you that your flight has been canceled."

"Ma'am, it's very simple," I said. "There are only three reasons on earth why anybody would ever cancel a flight to Dallas. Number one, something is wrong with that airplane, or number two, something is wrong with the person who's going to fly that airplane, or number three, something is wrong way up there. Now, ma'am, if any one of those three situations exists, I don't want to be up there. I want to be right down here. Fantastic."

Have you ever noticed that some people can't wait to give you the bad news? "Aw, Sally, I hate to tell you this. It just kills me to tell you this," and they can't wait to get the bad news out.

The lady put her hands on her hips and said, "Yeah, but the next flight doesn't leave until 6:05."

"Fantastic," I said.

By now, the people in the other two lines were looking over at me as if to say, "Who is that nut that says everything is fantastic?"

This brought the gate agent to a dead stop. She looked at me and said, "Now, look. I just told you that you have a four-hour wait here in the Kansas City airport, and you say fantastic. Now why on earth would you say a thing like that?"

"Ma'am, it's very simple," I said. "I'm fifty-four years old, and in my lifetime, I have never before had an opportunity to spend four hours in the airport in Kansas City. Do you realize at this precise moment, there are tens of millions of people on the face of this earth who are not only cold but hungry? Though it is awfully cold on the outside, here I am in a marvelously warm building. There's a nice little coffee shop down the way. I'm going to go down there, get myself a cup of coffee, and relax for a minute. Then I have some extremely important work I have to do.

Now here I am in one of the most beautiful buildings in the Kansas City area, with four hours of rent-free space, and I am really excited about it."

Now you might be thinking, "Ziglar, I've heard about these positive thinkers, but man, that's way out. Are you telling me the truth? Are you absolutely sure that's exactly what you said?"

Scout's honor, that is exactly what I said, and my son-in-law will validate that statement. Then you may say, "OK, OK, you said it, but now tell me the truth, Ziglar. Is that the way you really felt?"

Of course not. I'd been gone all week. I was tired, I wanted to be headed home, but you see, there are some things that we absolutely are not going to change in our life. I had a choice there. I didn't know that lady, but I knew that although she could cancel my flight, she couldn't cancel my day.

Did I want to respond, or did I want to react? I could have reacted sarcastically. I could have said, "That's just great. I've had my seat reserved now for over a month. As I drove up here, I could not help but notice a whole bunch of your airplanes sitting out there on the runway, not doing a cotton-picking thing. How come you can't crank up one of those airplanes and take me on down to Dallas with the other folks that want to go to Dallas?"

I could have done that. The next flight still would have left at 6:05.

I could have jumped up and down, ranted, raved, screamed, stomped my foot, and made an idiot out of myself: "I'll sue you, that's what I'll do to you. You hear me? I will sue you for the dastardly deed that you are pulling here." The next flight would still have left at 6:05.

Now, folks, there are some things you ain't going to change. If you were born white, you're going to stay white. If you were born black, you're going to stay black. You're not going to change one whisper about yesterday. Tomorrow, however, is an entirely different story, and whether you respond or react really does determine exactly what is going to happen in your life.

As I said, that lady could cancel my flight. She could not cancel my day. You know how folks are. You let them cancel today, and the first thing you know, they'll want to cancel two days, and then three days, and then four. Some people permit others to cancel their entire lifetimes. I've seen it happen.

Do you respond to life, or do you react to life? That is an enormously important message we need to understand.

Have you ever been riding down the freeway, minding your own business? You're neither positive nor negative, you're just riding along, and all of a sudden some idiot pulls in front of you.

You hit your brakes, you hit your horn at the same time, and you proceed to give him a piece of your mind. "Why don't you watch where you're going, you dummy? I could have hit you, and I could have been killed, and you could have been dead too. I'll tell you, your life is not safe anymore." You really read him the riot act.

You get down to your office, and what do you do? You tell the first person you meet about these crazy people out there on the freeway, and you tell the second person and the third person too. "He must have been drunk or on drugs or something. Your life is not safe out there anymore."

In the meantime, the man who did the dastardly deed rides merrily along, unaware of the fact that you even exist. Yet he's in control of your thinking, which means he's in control of your actions. He is affecting your relationship with those below you, above you, and around you, which means he is in control of your career, and you don't even know who he is. It is the ultimate putdown.

Do you respond or do you react to life? Your self-image is the key to which of these you do. Are you threatened by every little thing that comes along, or do you respond to that situation?

Several years ago, I went over to the bank out in North Dallas, and as I was pulling out into the flow of traffic, I heard the screeching of brakes and the shriek of an extraordinarily big horn, and I hit my brakes as quickly as I could. I looked up just in time to see a dude come steaming by in a big, old Mercedes.

If that look could have killed, there'd have been a funeral in Dallas a couple of days later. If it could have melted steel, I would have needed a new automobile. I'll tell you, I have never seen such a high concentration of ugly in one spot in my life. When that dude looked at me, he was upset.

I had a choice. I could have looked at him and said, "Why don't you watch where you're going, you dummy? I could have been killed. Come on back here, and we'll talk about this thing." I could have done that. Suppose he had. Suppose he had come back, gotten out, and whipped me.

Now, folks, it's kind of funny, yet it's tragically serious. Every day of our life in America, people are killed for less reason than that.

I had a choice: do I respond to what has just happened, or do I react? As he rode past, I looked up at him, and I said, "Hi." The guy did another take, and he gave a big smile. He waved his hand back at me, and was probably thinking to himself, "Boy, I almost blew it. That must be a friend of mine."

I believe that it is infinitely more important to respond than to react, and it is going to play a major role in how you get along with your mate, your children, your boss, your employees, your neighbors, and everybody else. The key is the image you have of yourself and your life. You cannot tailor-make the situations in life, but you can tailor-make your attitude in advance to fit those situations. That attitude, as I said, rests purely on the picture you have of yourself.

What does this story have to do with your self-image? It has everything to do with it. Reacting breeds anger. It breeds depression. It brings negativism and bitterness. Responding breeds hope and creativity, and it breeds action.

I'd like to give two classic examples of what I'm talking about. One is of a person who responded, and the other is of a person who reacted.

A number of years ago, a lady who had been doing a marvelous job with a particular company had a little problem with management. For whatever reason, they suddenly decided that they needed to serve drinks—cocktails, beer, wine, and so forth—at their meetings, particularly at their regional and national conventions.

She protested very strongly, because she knew the destructiveness of alcohol, and her belief system said, "This is not a good idea." She was the one who had built that sales organization. But she resisted serving alcohol so strongly, and management got so unhappy with her that one morning, when she awakened to get up and go to her job, she looked out on the front porch, and there was her desk. After a number of years, she had been summarily fired.

That's a pretty drastic action for somebody to take. Now the woman had a choice. Should she respond or react to that particular situation?

The woman quickly analyzed the situation, realized that she had already built that organization, which was doing millions of dollars' worth of business, and decided that she could do exactly the same thing for herself. She started a similar company. It was very difficult, because in those years, bankers did not believe in lending money to women, especially ones who didn't think you ought to drink.

This woman had some other weird ideas. For example, she thought you ought to pay your bills on time. She thought the customer ought to get a good deal, the salespeople ought to get a good deal, and the company still ought to be able to make a profit. She had a tough time getting along, but she hung in there, because she knew that she was born to win.

Eventually this company went on to in excess of $600 million worth of business. The lady I'm talking about is Mary Crowley. The company I'm talking about is Home Interiors & Gifts. She responded to the situation; she did not react. Responding is important. It's the direct reflection of the picture you have of yourself.

In the other case, I was once in a meeting where a very strong and successful businessman started talking about his childhood during World War II. His daddy had gone off to war, and while he was gone, his mother and aunt had—according to his father when he came home—made a sissy out of their little boy.

The father got a traveling job, and every Friday evening, he would come in and demand a list of all of the sins and crimes this little guy had committed in that week. One by one, he would go down the list, so the youngster started fearing when his dad would return home.

On one memorable occasion when the boy was in the first grade, a bully jumped him on the way to school and beat him up. He came home crying. His daddy said to him, "If you're going to act like girl, I'm going to dress you like a girl." He put a dress on him and sent him back out to fight the bully.

As I sat there listening to this man, the tears were streaming down his cheeks. He said, "I believe—I don't believe, I *know*—that that's been one reason that I became an alcoholic." But then he said, "Long ago, I dealt with this issue. I know that my daddy did not treat me that way because he hated me. My daddy treated me that way because he loved me. That's exactly the way he had been raised. That was the only thing that he knew. I've been able to deal with it and put it behind me."

Let me inject an important point here. Most people do what they do, not because they want to hurt somebody else, but because they're acting on the best information they have at the time. When we understand that, it makes forgiveness easier.

Of these two people, the woman, Mary Crowley, responded. The gentleman initially reacted, with disastrous results. Learning how to respond to what life brings us is enormously important.

One of the most beautiful letters I've ever gotten was from psychologist Dr. Jocelyn Fuller. She had attended a sales seminar, and she said, "You know, I never realized that salespeople are such good psychologists. I learned some things at that seminar that I never dreamed I would. I learned to appreciate my own profession more. Since then, I no longer have to parade my credentials. I no longer have to tell about my academic background. I still have them up on the wall, but I value myself for who I am, and not because of some piece of paper or a degree."

I work with a psychologist named Dr. John Leto. Dr. Leto says that if we learned to deal with everyone as if they were our best friend, we would be able to get along with and be accepted by far more people, and as a result our own self-image would be substantially improved.

I know it's awfully tough to respond when your mate of seventeen years walks out and leaves you with four children to raise. That doesn't get solved in twenty minutes. I know it's tough to respond when a trusted partner and friend embezzles funds from the company and forces you into bankruptcy, so that you lose your home and many other things.

I know it's tough to respond when you're unjustly fired, when you were abused as a child, or when your child was killed by a drunken driver or by a drive-by shooting, and the culprit walks away scot-free.

These things are awfully tough, but the question is how you respond. What steps do you take? First of all, you must acknowledge where you are. That's something we don't want to think about a lot of the time. Where am I at this moment? Where are you when something like that happens? I'm here to tell you we grow in adversity. Mary Crowley grew in adversity. You can grow in adversity.

There was an article in *Parade* magazine about a young man from Fort Worth named Randy Souders. He was seventeen years old, an athlete, a very healthy, outgoing young man. He injured himself in a diving accident and became a paraplegic. He was in the hospital for five months, and of course he was very upset about what had happened. One day, he's active and enthusiastic and doing everything that a healthy seventeen-year-old athlete would do. The next moment, he realizes he's going to be in a wheelchair for the rest of his life. He had a pity party going on there for about five months.

In the past, Randy had demonstrated some artistic skills. A therapist at the hospital forced a brush into his hand, so he again started doing some work in the world of art.

Randy's original objective had been to get into creative advertising. While he was piddling with his artwork, he went to work with an ad agency, and one of his pictures was sitting on the floor. A gentleman saw it and said, "Hey, do you have another picture like that? Do you have any that are for sale?"

Six years later, this young man had developed a talent that enabled his paintings to be in over fifteen hundred galleries around the country. He said, "Had this accident not happened to me, I doubt that I would be where I am today."

Randy took the proverbial lemon and made the proverbial lemonade. He took what happened to him, moaned for a few months, and then decided he had to get on with life.

People have asked Randy, "Do you think about that wheelchair all the time?"

He responds, "The last thing I ever think about is my wheelchair when I get up in the morning. I'm excited about what I'm doing."

When we get excited about life, we can respond instead of reacting. Understand where you are. Take a little inventory. If you're feeling down, if you really are not happy with things, it's OK.

Years ago *The New York Times* published a very significant article. It pointed out that a lot of people have every reason to be negative and pessimistic. Maybe their lives up until this point have indicated that that's where they ought to be. But once you've identified where you are, don't go around beating yourself up about it. Start looking at how you can change your thinking. When you change your thinking, you change your action. When you change your action, you change your future.

How do you change your thinking? You change what you put in your mind. Your mind is the gateway to the heart. You're what you are and where you are because of what's gone into that mind. You can change what you are and where you are by changing what goes into your mind.

I love the story of the old Eskimo up in Alaska who had two fighting dogs. One was white, and one was black. He brought them to town every Saturday.

In those days, they had vicious dogfights. One Saturday the white dog would win; one Saturday the black dog would win.

The dogs were vicious and cruel, and after a period of time, they had chewed each other up so much that they no longer could put on a good fight, so the Eskimo retired them.

One Saturday, he was back in town, and somebody asked him, "You know, I noticed that the white dog won one week, and the black dog won one week, but I also noticed that 100 percent of the time, you bet on the dog that won. How on earth did you know every week which one was going to win?"

The old Eskimo smiled and said, "Well, it really was pretty easy. I always bet on the one I'd been feeding all week." It doesn't take a genius to figure that one out, does it?

Nor does it take a genius to figure out that what we put in our mind affects our thinking, and our thinking affects our actions, and our actions affect our future? The major message: acknowledge where you are.

The second thing to do, if you believe that someone is responsible for your dilemma in life, then you ought to get rip-roaring, snorting mad about it. Get absolutely furious, and blame them for everything that's gone wrong in your life.

Write this person a barn burner of a letter. Express every emotion you have; say, "You rascal, you shouldn't have done this. You dirty dog, this was wrong, and I'm furious with you for doing it. You made a mess out of my life, and I'm mad, mad, mad." Let it all hang out.

Put the letter aside for a few hours, then get it back out. Reread it to make certain you've included everything. If you have to add a PS, or even three or four, add them all. Read the letter over carefully. It might be ten or twelve pages. Make certain that you've gotten it all out.

Now you take that letter, go outside, and take a page. Say, "You dirty dog, you shouldn't have done it," but burn the page and say, "I'm going to forget about it. I'm going to forgive you for this." Burn the next page, and say, "I forgive you for this." Burn the next page, and say, "I forgive you for this." Burn the next page, and say, "I forgive you for this," and so on.

Let me emphasize one point. When a lot of crimes have been committed, especially incest, sexual abuse, and verbal abuse, and they've been brutalized over a long period of time, some people find it absolutely impossible to forgive them without some help. I encourage you to get counseling, because forgiveness is absolutely critical. You must forgive them for what they have done.

You might argue, "That so-and-so doesn't deserve to be forgiven." I would agree with you, but let God be the decider in that issue. Don't play God. Let God forgive them; let God deal with them. You need to forgive that person for your own benefit.

That might take counseling, and in many cases, it absolutely will take counseling, but let me add that I do not recommend that you go and confront that person, particularly at this stage of the game. Don't be vindictive. Physician Hans Selye says, "The healthiest human emotion is gratitude, and the most destructive is revenge."

Do not do anything that would hurt the other person. Remember, you have forgiven them. Although I have said to forget what has happened, in many cases, this is impossible, because everything we've ever seen, heard, smelled, tasted, touched, or thought about has become a part of us. Rather, when I say forget it, you forget that you're going to extract vengeance on them. You give up the right to extract revenge from them. It's tough to do, but it's enormously important.

Actually this process is extremely dangerous to do.

When you've been blaming somebody else for your problems all of your life, and all of a sudden you forgive them, you can no longer blame them. That means you're now accepting responsibility for your future. That's the most important step you will ever take: accepting that responsibility. Nonetheless, you'll discover that the load is so much lighter that you can move much faster.

The Roman emperor and philosopher Marcus Aurelius put it this way: "How much more grievous are the consequences of anger than the causes of it."

I love what author Bill O'Hearn says in one of his little books: imagine in life that you're given so many grams or ounces or BTUs of energy. When all the energy is gone, that's the end of your life. Also suppose that every time you love somebody or are nice to somebody, you're given an extra portion of energy.

Then, he said, imagine that every time you seek revenge or let anger control your life, a double portion of that energy is burned. You're shortening your own life. Incidentally, that's exactly what doctors say as well.

You need to learn to forgive. In our society today, we not only need forgiveness, but we need to develop a little sense of humor to go along with it.

I love the story of the lady who went in the grocery store and ordered a twenty-five-pound turkey. The butcher said, "We don't have a twenty-five-pounder, but I can get one for you."

"No," said the woman. "I didn't want to buy it. I just wanted to look at it."

"Why would you want to look at a twenty-five-pound turkey?"

"I've been on a diet, and I've just lost twenty-five pounds. I wanted to see what it looked like in one spot."

I believe that we need to learn to laugh at a lot of things. We also need to remember that the strong and the wise admit they have weaknesses. It's an indication of a healthy self-image.

It doesn't bother me that I can't perform an appendectomy. As a matter of fact, there are over fifty thousand ways to earn a living in America that I don't know how to do. Why should we get concerned about what we cannot do? Why not concentrate on the things we can do, including admitting our weaknesses? Let me give you some examples.

If you had a broken leg, you wouldn't hesitate to go to the doctor to get it fixed. If you had a serious drinking problem, if you were wise and strong, you would admit you could not handle it. You would seek help of some kind through Alcoholics Anonymous (AA) or any number of other sources, but you'd say, "Hey, I have a problem I can't solve. Would you help me?" A lot of times, counseling with a godly counselor will help you to forgive a person if you cannot handle it yourself. Let me offer another example.

My son Tom and his wife, Chachis, had gotten on various eating and exercise programs before. Tom needed to lose about forty-five pounds, and he'd been on and off and on and off. He went to see Dr. Cooper, who'd been a friend of mind for many years and had been so helpful to me. Tom checked out to find out exactly where he was, and then he joined a health club and hired a trainer.

Why would he hire a trainer? You can learn what to do, but do you sometimes know what to do and still don't do it? Have you ever turned in a report or a paper in school when you didn't really want to, but you knew the teacher demanded and expected it, so you showed up with a paper?

Until the habit becomes a permanent part of us, we often flat-out need somebody to assist us in our discipline. Tom needed to lose weight. Chachis, on the other hand, needed to gain some weight, and she needed to get stronger. They both hired a trainer.

For the first few weeks, they'd come in saying, "I'm so tired. I'm so sore," but they knew that was going to happen. They had made the commitment. In the end, Chachis gained seven pounds and got considerably stronger, and her energy level dramatically improved. Tom has lost over forty pounds, and his energy level was higher too. Guess what that also did to their self-images.

Tom and Chachis had a problem. They said, "I can't solve it. Won't you help?" A good, healthy self-image will let you do that.

You also need to forgive yourself. That too might take counseling. In cases of sexual abuse, notably incest, the victim is often persuaded by the perpetrator that it's all the victim's fault. Let me give you this assurance: if you were a child when that happened, there is nothing on earth you could have done to prevent it. There is nothing you could have done to stop it. If you have any guilt feelings, it is because the perpetrator planted those feelings of guilt and fear as the incidents were taking place. If you cannot forgive yourself, you need to go and get some counseling and get that forgiveness.

How important is your self-image? Let's play a game. Let's pretend that one morning, as you're getting ready to go to work, the telephone rings, and the voice at the other end says, "Charlie, I hope I didn't wake you up, and I don't want to slow you down from getting to work on time, but I've been thinking about you, and I just wanted to call you and tell you how much I admire and respect you. You're the kind of person that I flat-out enjoy being around. When I'm with you, I'm always encouraged and enthused.

"Charlie, if there were more people like you, we would have a much better world to live in. If I could spend five minutes a day with you, I'd be able to turn this world upside down. Man, I hope you live a long, happy, and prosperous life so you can encourage other people as you encourage me. That's all I wanted to say, Charlie. Talk to you later," and he hangs up.

This call was from a close friend, so you knew he was sincere. Here's my question: what kind of day would you have after you got this call? Would it be a pretty good day? If you were a salesperson out making sales calls, would you be more enthusiastic, more persuasive, and more committed? Would you do a better job that day? If you were a physician, would you be a better physician? If you were an attorney, would you be a better attorney? If you were a school-teacher, would you be a better teacher? If you were a mom or a dad, would you be a better parent?

Of course you would. Let me tell you why. You'd say, "I'm an asset to my community. I'm a credit to my profession. That old boy said so, and he is one smart cookie."

Your friend would have taught you nothing about being a better salesperson, a better doctor, or a better parent. Nevertheless, you would be better at all of these things, because the picture you have of yourself, your attitude toward yourself, would have undergone a substantial change. When that happens, performance goes up.

How do you change your self-image? Let's look at some specific steps. Eleanor Roosevelt said that no one on earth can make you feel inferior without your permission. So promise yourself that never again will you permit anybody else to make you feel less about yourself. I cannot state this point strongly enough. It is important.

I love the story of a little guy whose self-image was pretty intact. The teacher required the class to talk about some exciting event that took place over the weekend. She called on Little Johnny first and said, "Johnny, what happened to you this weekend?"

"Oh, teacher, it was wonderful," said Little Johnny. "My dad took me fishing. We caught seventy-five catfish, and each one of them weighed seventy-five pounds."

The teacher said, "Now, Johnny, you know that could not possibly be true."

"Oh, yes, it is."

"Now, Johnny, I know that that cannot be. What would you think of me if I said to you that on the way to school this morning, I was confronted by a thousand-pound grizzly bear? He was just about to jump on me and eat me up when an itty-bitty dog that weighed about three pounds came up to him. The dog jumped up, grabbed the grizzly bear by the nose, threw him down, and shook him until it killed him. Johnny, what would you think about that? Would you believe it?"

"Yes, ma'am, I sure would," said Little Johnny. "As a matter of fact, that is my dog."

I would say that his self-image was OK.

How does your image affect your performance? How does the way you see other people affect their performance?

When our daughter, Julie, was in the fifth grade, the teacher came to us and said, "Julie is an average student. She'll make Cs primarily. She'll make an occasional B and an occasional D, but don't worry about it. She's very personable, she makes a lot of friends, but don't be too hard on her if she's not a top performer."

We never told our little girl she was a C student. Nor did the teacher, but because you treat people exactly as you see them, I'm certain that in a thousand different ways we communicated to Julie, "We expect a C performance out of you."

At one point, after having been out of school for something like seventeen years, Julie went back to school. During her first semester, she carried sixteen very tough hours, including two very difficult labs. She made the dean's list. She came within a whisper of a 4.0 average.

One night I called her house and spoke to her husband. After we had chatted, I said, "Let me speak to Julie." He started laughing.

"What are you laughing about?" I asked.

"Julie's next door teaching Diane advanced math."

He was laughing about that because for a great part of her life, she had been hearing that old refrain: "I just can't learn math. I just can't learn math." Yet here she was, teaching advanced math to a neighbor.

What had happened? She explained it to me: "Dad, I discovered that knowledge reveals itself to anyone who diligently pursues it. I had never really mastered the formulas, and when I learned those formulas, math is a snap. It is easy."

Quite possibly ten or more years after you finished your formal education, you decided to go back and get more education. It's also quite possible that when you went back, you did better, maybe substantially better, than when you'd been in school the first time.

If so, let me tell you why. You planned to do better, you prepared to do better, you expected to do better, and you went back at your own expense. It's called *commitment*. Furthermore, over the years, you had learned that you are a bright, productive person. The picture you had of yourself, as well as your ambition to go back, says a lot about you. When the image changes, the performance is absolutely going to change.

The *Los Angeles Times* once ran a substantial article about a study of people who were enormously successful. At one stage of their lives, these people had made a deliberate choice to associate with a different crowd. Apparently the crowd you associate with has something to do with your accomplishments in life.

Today we have an entirely different crowd that is influencing many. It is an income suppressant that some people refer to as *television*. Think about the crowds you run with when you look at television: murders, drive-by shootings, violence, rapists, racists: you see absolutely everything there. When you associate with those people, when mom and dad sit and watch these things with their children, they're tacitly saying that it's OK to cuss, it's OK to be violent, it's OK to get drunk. Watching those things actually encourages participation.

The tragedy is, television could be enormously helpful. It dramatizes things so powerfully that it would be beneficial if they chose the right things.

Watch the people you associate with. Watch what goes on in your mind; it affects your thinking. Your thinking affects your performance. Your performance reflects back your image.

To improve your image, improve your memory. How many times have you bragged about having a lousy memory? Have you ever said, "I can remember faces, but I cannot remember names"? When you repeat that over and over, it's like my daughter with math. It becomes a reality.

I don't necessarily believe that everybody needs to know how to remember three hundred people right after they met them, but I'm going to tell you a little story.

We teach a three-day seminar called "Born to Win." One year, we were doing a portion on memory in that seminar.

A fellow named Dan Clarke and his wife, Kelly, from Salt Lake City attended. He was the all-American football player—big defensive end, good-looking guy, outstanding speaker. She was a beauty queen, a gorgeous, wonderfully personable, sweet individual. That was a match. You'd say, "Those two really do go together."

We had a hundred people there, and the memory teacher that day was giving out points if participants got the first and last name of every person there. In the little test that followed, Kelly was number one. She only missed one out of a possible two hundred.

We gave out little awards, so when Kelly stepped up to receive hers, she broke down and wept. She said, "All of my life, I thought I was dumb. I just learned in the last hour and a half that I'm a very bright person."

This has a double point. There are a lot of good memory books and techniques from which you can learn in order to improve your self-image and give you added confidence. But what I'm really talking about is growth. Every time you take a step forward, every time you learn something of value, it tends to improve the picture. You need to keep growing.

Football player and sportscaster Terry Bradshaw says, "The life of a winner is the result of an unswerving commitment to a never-ending process of self-completion."

The question that is most often asked of my staff and my family is, "Is Zig really up like that all the time?" Well, let me tell you, folks, I *am* up, but there is a difference between being up and being on.

If you're on 100 percent of the time, folks, you're doing something that's going to end up killing you. The only time I really get down is when I am physically exhausted. Years ago I learned I do not make important decisions when I'm physically exhausted.

When I finish a three- or four-hour seminar, I'm exhausted.

At these points, I will go home, and my wife— whom I call the redhead—will have lunch for me. We'll eat and visit for about an hour, and then I will take a nap for about thirty or forty minutes. When I get up, I will take a casual walk for about thirty minutes, and then I will take a fast walk for about thirty minutes, and I'll be ready to go again. That's the way I stay up the overwhelming majority of the time.

The second thing I do is practice what I preach. I read for three hours a day and have for twenty years. But maybe the most significant thing is that when I speak, I'm the one who's listening more carefully than anybody else. This is my self-talk. When I'm saying to you, "This is what you ought to do," I'm saying, "Yeah, Ziglar, that sounds like a good idea, man. Do it yourself." To the very best of my ability, I do exactly what I am telling you to do.

How do you build your self-image? Remember that failure is an event; it is not a person. A musician hits a sour note. Does that mean he's a failure as a musician? A student misses a question. Does that mean she's a failure as a student? The cook burns the beans. Does that mean he's a failure as a cook? The salesperson misses a sale. Does that mean that that salesperson is a failure? You take a wrong turn on the highway. Does that mean you're an idiot, or does it simply mean you made a wrong turn? When the quarterback throws past the wide receiver, does that mean he's a failure as a quarterback, or does it simply mean that on that particular occasion, he happened to make a mistake?

I don't believe I can say too many times that failure is an event. It is not a person. Yesterday did end last night. Today is a brand-new day, and it's yours.

I love the story told of the thirty-year-old scrubwoman who was on welfare. To quote her, she had been born ugly, and then somebody scared her. She was not a beauty contest winner. As she was pondering her welfare and floor scrubbing job, she started doing a little personal evaluation. She picked up a book entitled *The Magic of Believing*. This book gave her a new picture of herself. It gave her new hope, and remember, if there's hope in the future, there's power in the present.

She remembered that when she had been in school, she had the ability to make people laugh. So she decided that she would start practicing on her friends and in social events. She started making people laugh, and over the years, Phyllis Diller earned millions of dollars making people laugh.

I'm here to tell you that we can change. We can grow. We can be more than we are. If you don't like who you are or where you are, don't sweat it. You're not stuck with who you are or where you are. You absolutely can grow. You can change.

How do you build a healthy self-image? Take inventory of yourself. How much money would you take for your health? Once a man named Barney Clark was given a mechanical heart implant. It cost several million dollars, but it only extended his life for a few weeks. If you have a good heart, then, how much is yours worth?

Once a lady went to a doctor about a rash on her face. He prescribed some drugs. They settled in her eyes, and she lost her sight. The insurance company gave her a check for a million dollars. What would you take for your eyes?

Similarly, a lady was injured in an airplane accident and lost her ability to walk. They gave her a million dollars. What would you take for your legs?

In the 1940s, actress Betty Grable was known for her legs. She had a beautiful face and nice arms, but her legs were insured for a million dollars. If your legs will let you move around, how much would you take for yours? When you begin to evaluate yourself, the figure really gets to be high.

Let me remind you of my friend John Foppe, who was born without any arms. He said to me, "You know, Zig, I can only do so much with arms, but I can do so many things with my mind."

When you take inventory, we really are extraordinarily well-off.

If you had a $50,000 automobile, and somebody said something ugly about it, you'd get upset: "What do you mean talking about this $50,000 car? Man, it's magnificent." Now *you* can say something ugly about your car, but you don't want anybody else to.

What about the billion-dollar you? You're fearfully and wonderfully made. Evaluate yourself. I'm not talking about a superinflated, "I am the greatest" ego. You know, conceit's a weird thing: it makes everybody sick except the one who has it. That's not what I'm talking about. I'm talking about a simple, healthy self-acceptance. To improve your self-image, you need to make up, dress up, and then you need to go up.

Saturday is one of the best days around my house. The redhead takes a trip every Saturday that we're in town, and she's gone about two hours. When she comes back, she's stepping a little bit higher, she's smiling a little bit more broadly, and she's a little more friendly.

Where's she been? To the beauty shop. I've never been able to figure what rearranging a few hairs on the head has to do with all that, but it really has a lot. Don't you feel more competent, more confident when you're sharp-looking?

When they have picture-taking days at school, they've found that the kids were better behaved and performed better on that day. When you look sharp, you feel sharp, and that makes you sharp. When you make up and dress up, your chances of going up are absolutely better.

How many of you remember the comic strip *Li'l Abner*, by Al Capp? I used to love Li'l Abner. My favorite character was General Bullmoose. He used to say, "If it's good for Bullmoose, it's good for the world." He had a good, healthy self-image, although unfortunately his went into egotism.

In Southern schools, they used to have a Sadie Hawkins Day, when everybody dressed up in raggedy clothes. After a few years, they stopped having them. Why? Violence, vandalism, poorer conduct, poorer performance were the direct result of looking like that.

When you make up and dress up, your chances of going up are definitely going to be improved. You need to get the bear out of the tree. What do I mean when I say that?

Years ago, in Keithville, Louisiana, they had an incredible amount of excitement. Late one Saturday afternoon, just as it was getting dark, somebody was riding through this little underbrush area. They looked up in the tree, and there was a black bear. Now a black bear up a tree close to Keithville, Louisiana, created a lot of excitement.

They notified everybody. The fire department came out. The police came out. A veterinarian came out, and everybody was there. They decided to let the veterinarian start shooting the bear with tranquilizer darts. They got the fire department there with a net to catch him when he fell out.

Well, they kept shooting that sucker, and he kept staying up there. They finally decided they'd just patiently wait all night, and they posted a lookout to see if any activity took place up there. Nothing happened.

The next morning, they still couldn't get him out. They decided that they were going to have to cut the tree down, because they didn't want that black bear running loose in the neighborhood. They cut the tree down, and they were prepared to do what they needed to do to make certain that he didn't get hurt or hurt anybody else. When the tree came down, they discovered it was a plastic bag filled with garbage.

There are an awful lot of people who have a bear up a tree. They have their pasts buried in their mind. They concentrate on the negatives of life. As a result, they end up never doing the things that they are capable of doing. Your self-image is enormously important.

TWO

Polish Your Self-Image

I t seems that a certain fellow was driving in what we'll call a nonprofessional manner. A police officer arrested him and took him to night court. As the man stood before the judge, the judge said, "OK, I want you to do a few things."

"Like what?"

"I want you to lift your hands straight up over your head."

"I can't do that."

"Why can't you?"

"I was injured in a skiing accident."

"OK. I want you to turn your head left and right."

"I can't do that."

"Why?"

"I was injured in a diving accident."

"OK. I want you to bend over and touch your toes."

"I can't do that."

"How come you can't?"

"I injured my back lifting."

"All right. I want you to stand on one leg."

"I can't do that."

"Why?"

"Because I'm drunk."

Then the judge said, "All right. That'll be $1,000 or ninety days. Which will you choose?"

"I'll take the $1,000." I would say he had great presence of mind.

What causes all of the image problems that we have? Why are the acknowledged beauties of Hollywood the envy of so many "average" people? Why do over 90 percent of people want to change the way they are? It is simply because they have a perception of their image. The beauty magazines, the fashion magazines, the articles that we read are constantly lauding beauty and health and brains.

Those things obviously could be assets or they could be liabilities, but we don't put enough emphasis on the things that really make a difference—character qualities.

In addition, there is so much negative input. Author Shad Helmstetter says that the typical sixteen-year-old has been told "no" or "you can't do it" 147,000 times. If you tell a youngster they can't do something 147,000 times, they are likely to believe it.

Parents often say, "You never do anything right. You're always late. That's dumb. You can't learn math." Think of the pictures that those statements make in the person's mind.

I'm convinced that the greatest damage, the greatest injustice, that has been done to the black man by his white brothers relates to self-image.

Now, I'm a child of the South; I was raised over in Mississippi. When I was a boy, I used to go to Shirley Temple movies, and I thought they were so cute. She was always dancing and singing, and she was Little Miss Perfect.

I vividly remember seeing one of her movies, but until Bill Cosby explained the movie through the eyes of a black man, I had no idea of the incredible damage that has been done.

Here's the scene: There's a birthday party. Little Miss Shirley is five years old. She has her friends around, and they're having their cake and ice cream at the party. It's just about over, and then a tall, slender African-American girl, who appears to be thirteen or fourteen years old, comes up to her, with two friends, who are much younger.

As they came up, they said, "Miss Shirley"—get that picture, a thirteen-year-old addressing a five-year-old—"we brought you a present."

Miss Shirley says, "Oh, thank you very much. Now you can have some of our leftover birthday cake."

The little black girl puts her hands over her eyes, and says, "Oh, Miss Shirley."

Can you see what that would do to the self-image of blacks? As a child, I'd watched that scene, but I'd never understood it before; I just thought it was cute. But hearing Bill Cosby explain it was one of the most eye-opening experiences I have ever had.

This story appeared in *Reader's Digest* a number of years ago: A salesman was on the streets of New York selling balloons. As the crowd grew smaller, he would release a balloon, maybe a white one. You know how people watch those things when they go up? Then people would gather around and buy again. In a few minutes he would release a red one, and the same thing would happen. Then he'd release a yellow one.

Presently a little African-American youngster walked up to him, tugged on his sleeve, and said, "Mister, if you released one of the black ones, would it go up?"

With a wisdom that you really would not expect to find in one who was selling balloons on the street, the man looked down at the youngster and said, "Son, it's what's inside of those balloons that makes them go up."

That's what we need to understand. It's what's inside that's going to make us go up. "Some of us," as my friend, psychologist Don Beck, says, "are packaged a little differently, but when we get inside, the heart and the mind are all exactly the same color."

One of the most impressive articles I've ever read was in the February 1992 issue of *Scientific American*. It was about some Indonesian immigrants in America. They had been in detention camps two or three years, so their educational process had been hampered.

These immigrants were put in the inner cities of America; five hundred students were involved in the study. The researchers discovered some interesting things. Number one, the larger the family, the better the students' grades. The older kids in the family were teaching the younger kids.

Number two, the researchers found that when the parents read to the students, whether it was in their native tongue or in English, their grades were absolutely fabulous. The researchers also discovered that when the immigrants reinforced their culture and their self-image by being proud of their heritage, their grades were affected as a direct result. Furthermore, when the parents and the teachers worked together, the results were magnificent.

This study centered around one particular group, but the article pointed out that right after World War II, when prejudice was at its very peak against the Japanese, Japanese students who were given exactly the same treatment at home and whose parents cooperated with the teachers showed the same results. They did a study of African-Americans in Chicago and discovered the same thing. The same with a study involving Jews. It doesn't make any difference which continent you're from or what the color of your skin is—the same treatment will produce the same results.

Now think with me. What would it do to the self-image of everyone to really understand that how you treat people has a bearing on their image? Their image in turn has a direct bearing on their performance.

Let me give you a tragic example of what happens when a youngster has a poor self-image and is rejected.

In March 1993, a fourteen-year-old from Haltom City, Texas, killed a policeman and seriously wounded three of his neighbors, even though his father was on the police force. The youngster was also killed as a result of the interchange of gunfire.

What brought this on? The boy's classmates called him a nerd. They made fun of his clothing. He did poorly in school. His parents disciplined him and made him stay at home and study on Saturday. Something apparently snapped. He reacted to what had happened with tragic results.

You have to wonder what would have happened in that youngster's life had even one student come to him and said, "I think you're a neat guy. I think you are an OK kid. I'd like to be your friend."

I'm not saying this to put a guilt trip on any of his classmates. You can't saw sawdust, you can't undo what has already happened, but we can learn from the lesson and prepare for the future.

I'm totally convinced that if this boy's self-image had been different, he would have been a different person. He'd been conditioned to believe that he was a failure. Negative conditioning is the mother of learning, the father of action, and the architect of failure. Positive conditioning is the mother of learning, the father of action, and the architect of success. Do you respond to life, or do you react to life?

Once when I was out in San Francisco doing a seminar, I went down to attend a football practice session at Los Gatos High School in Los Gatos, California. The coach was the late Charlie Wedemeyer. The practice session was fascinating.

Charlie and I spent about an hour and a half together talking, but about every three minutes, one of the assistant coaches would come running up and say, "Charlie, they're trap-blocking us every time on that play. What do we do?" Immediately Charlie would give them an answer.

A few minutes later, another coach would come back to him and say, "Charlie, that guy is beating us around the end every time. What can we do?" Charlie would give them an answer. He had been watching intently and listening just as intently. He led his team to the only state championship they have ever won.

Now the fascinating thing is that Charlie Wedemeyer could not talk. As a matter of fact, he had Lou Gehrig's disease. The only parts of his body that could even move were his eyelids and his mouth. His vocal cords were paralyzed. Nothing came out; only his lips moved. His wife, Lucy, read his lips and communicated the message to whoever was there.

I'd never seen anybody with a healthier self-image. Here was a guy who, in the seventies, was the athlete of the decade in Hawaii. He was a superb physical specimen in every way before he fell victim to that disease, but he understood that his value was not wrapped up in what he could do physically.

Charlie was an inspiration. He had one of the greatest senses of humor I have ever dealt with. He traveled a lot. It was difficult, with the equipment they had to haul with him, taking the nurse, and taking his wife, and so forth, but he frequently went to address high schools and prisons. He made a statement, and then Lucy repeated it.

Charlie was honored in 1992 as the Disabled American of the Year. President George H. W. Bush was supposed to attend the session, but at the last minute had to cancel. When Charlie made his talk (obviously with Lucy doing all the talking), he said he was very sorry that the president couldn't be there, because he'd been planning to say to him, "Read my lips." He had responded rather than reacting to what had happened to him.

Now let me ask you a question: do you honestly believe that the works of Abraham Lincoln, Helen Keller, Martin Luther King Jr., Moses, Confucius, Mahatma Gandhi, and Jesus Christ have had a positive influence, not only on America but on the world?

If so, do you believe that the input of a Prince or a Madonna or 2 Live Crew or Ice-T could have a negative influence on our behavior and what we do in America?

You may remember the sex books that Madonna put out. I think 700,000 or 800,000 copies were sold very quickly, at $50 a throw. Time Warner only put two restrictions on her: she could not use a religious object to have sex with in the pictures, and she could not have sex with an animal.

Now let me ask you a question. Will that build the kind of America that can solve its multitrillion-dollar deficit? Will that build a kind of America that will solve our crime problem, bring our families back together, and make our streets safe to walk on? What do you think?

If we acknowledge that good input produces good results, then we cannot deny that improper input will produce improper and undesirable results.

Let me give you one of the great truths of life: you, or the people you talk to, might not believe everything you say, but I can guarantee you they're going to believe everything that you do.

Be careful about what you put in your mind. Suppose you were told over and over, "You're a winner. You can do it. You're a marvelous human being. Here's why." Suppose that over and over you were told of all the good things you could do. Would that have a positive influence on you?

Suppose you were told over and over, "You're a dummy. You can't do it. It's OK to fight somebody," and that sort of stuff. Do you believe that could have a negative influence on your life? I think the point is pretty well made.

The *Dallas Morning News* of March 10, 1993 had a substantial article about the damage that is done to people's self-image when we compare ourselves to the glamorous and brilliant people of the world.

Does that constitute success? Actually, millionaires are boring. You'll probably be surprised to know that there are far more salespeople who are millionaires than doctors. There are countless millionaires in America with average jobs. According to *U.S. News and World Report*, fewer than one percent of all of the millionaires in America are in athletics, entertainment, music, television, and the movies combined. The other 99 percent are people like you and me who hung in there over a period of time. We need to get a different picture of ourselves.

What causes a poor self-image? Poverty can be a cause. For example, if a home is such that the child is unwilling to bring their friends there, that has an impact. If the child has a parent who is a drunk or a drug addict and is embarrassed to introduce people to them, that can give them a poor self-image.

Harsh, brutal treatment, physical abuse, verbal abuse all have an impact, but the number one cause of a poor self-image is a lack of unconditional love. You accept and love your child, not because they made an A, not because they cleaned their room, not because they made their bed, not because they're in on time, but because they are yours and you unconditionally accept them as yours.

As I've mentioned, one of the most destructive things for self-image has to do with incest or sexual abuse. (Incidentally, for what it's worth, when a single mother who has a little girl invites her boyfriend to come live with her, she has just extended an invitation to the neighborhood pedophile. This happens too many times to be a coincidence.)

What causes poor self-image? Media treatment today. Have you ever noticed the way they treat two-parent families, or people who have religious convictions? When was the last time you saw a series that had a regular husband and wife as the heroes of the series? Most of the time, the father is either brutal or a wimp. Too much of the time, the children make old dad look like an idiot, and the kids are smarter than mom and dad put together. That creates a real problem.

It pains me to say this, but negative preachers are one of the biggest causes of a negative self-image—the ones who talk about nothing but hell and brimstone. Now don't misunderstand; I think some of that ought to be there, but we need to look at the positive side as well.

Exploring the manifestations of a poor self-image will help us identify the people we're dealing with, and hopefully ourselves. If we can tell that a person has a given problem, and if we have the same kind of problem, we're in a position to offer a solution.

One manifestation of a poor self-image is jealousy without cause. Many times a husband or wife will say, "I just love them so much, I can't let them out of my sight." They're really saying, "I cannot believe he or she would be faithful to poor little old me."

The second manifestation of a poor self-image is a failure to give your best effort. If you don't, you can always say, "If I'd really tried, I would have succeeded in that endeavor." You have a fear that if you'd really tried but failed, your self-image would deteriorate further. As a result, people don't finish projects, whether it's cutting the grass or getting the report in on time.

When you finish, you get recognition, you get praise. So such people think, "I don't deserve praise, so if I don't finish the project, I won't get praise." They may not think this through consciously, but instinctively that's what happens.

People with a poor self-image are afraid that others are laughing at them. If they leave a gathering before it's broken up, they'll ask later, "What were you all talking about? Did you mention me?" They're overly sensitive to criticism. They can't handle a compliment. If someone says, "Boy, I'm telling you, this is one of the most delicious casseroles I've ever eaten," they'll reply, "I wish I'd had time to marinate the veal a little bit longer."

Or if someone says, "My, that's a beautiful dress you have on," they'll say, "I've been wearing it for there years, but thank you."

Or if they're told, "My, your house is always so neat," they'll say, "I wish I'd had more time to take care of some of the panels."

People with a poor self-image cannot accept a simple compliment and say thank you, which is a sign of a good, healthy self-image. Or they may insist on picking up the check at a meal, even though they cannot afford it. They believe they're not worthy of your company unless they give you something, so they pick up the check.

People of this kind advertise themselves by dressing in revealing clothes. Fishermen call that trolling. The only problem with trolling is that sometimes you pick up an old boot or a stump, and you find out that it's tougher to get it off the hook than it was to get it on.

Salespeople with poor self-images will fail to ask for the order. For fifteen years, I was in direct sales. I've seen hundreds of efforts by salespeople to close the sale. They'll be talking and talking without ever asking for the order. Finally, the prospect says, "Well, John, you're not trying to sell me something, are you?"

"Oh, no, no."

What are you then, a professional visitor?

We've discovered that sales escalate dramatically when the self-image improves, because when you have the right image, you're selling the right product. If you feel good about yourself and what you're selling, you want the other person to own it for their benefit, not yours.

Another manifestation of a poor self-image is overpromising. We've all seen it. A new coach comes in and says, "It might take a rebuilding process, but I can guarantee you it's going to be a lot faster than a lot of people think." They overpromise. Politicians are notoriously famous for that, are they not? They overpromise because they are afraid they won't be accepted unless they do.

The old motormouth is one sign of a poor self-image. People of this kind talk all the time. They simply can never slow down because they feel they always have to be selling and selling.

Have you ever paid a short visit on a motormouth? After about fifteen minutes, it's time to go. As you head for the front door, he blocks it off; he stands in the way; he has something else to tell you. You finally maneuver to get out the door, and he follows you out to the car. He opens the door for you, and as you're backing out, he says, "Roll down the window. I have one more thing to tell you." In many cases the class clown is another type of individual who has a poor self-image.

Sometimes a silent mouth is also a sign of a poor self-image—not always, but sometimes. These people are simply afraid that what they have to say is of very little value; consequently, they do not say anything.

Of course, a filthy mouth is one of the surest give-aways of all. These people think that in order to get somebody to listen, they have to punctuate their talk with obscene comments. One of the advice col-umnists—Ann Landers or Dear Abby—did a survey and found that 99 percent of the people in America believe that TV and movies play down to us, and we're offended by a lot of the language used. What can we do about it? Hey, don't watch them. That's one thing we can do.

Interestingly, even a golf ball can be a sign of a poor self-image. I found one once when I was out walking. It was out of bounds. It was a brand new Titleist, and on it was written, "Strike three." Does that tell you something? Does that say this was an individual who had painted a picture in his mind of himself as a lousy golfer, who was thinking, "I know what I'm going to do. I'm going to strike out again"?

These same manifestations of a poor self-image occur in other professions and areas of life. The student with a poor self-image, for example, will never confront the teacher over a grade, even when he knows he deserves a better one. He won't ask the pretty girl for a date, because in his mind, he doesn't deserve such a girl. The tragedy is, she probably wanted to go out with him.

The office worker with a self-image problem won't assert herself and ask for a raise even when she knows that the caliber of her work warrants more pay. Unfortunately, if the worker doesn't get the raise and recognition she deserves, she will become resentful and feel that no one understands or appreciates her. The net result is a negative effect on her performance and a reduced possibility of a future raise.

The husband or wife with a poor self-image becomes a doormat for the other one. They never quietly, sanely, reasonably raise questions or say, "Here's what I think. Have you explored this? Have you looked at the other side?" That doesn't make for a good relationship.

There's evidence that the good old Joe (and his female counterpart) has a problem that has nothing to do with age, sex, education, size, or skin color. He has the syndrome of thinking, "I must be a nice guy and never offend anyone." As a youngster, he smokes cigarettes he doesn't want, takes the drink he doesn't like, laughs at dirty jokes that actually offend him, joins the gang he dislikes, and goes along with conduct and dress that he secretly abhors.

One survey about drinking at colleges, reported in *USA Today*, said that many of the students who get drunk do so because they think that everybody expects them to and that it will make them more acceptable. But the survey proved beyond any doubt that they actually go down in the estimation of others, so they are acting on a false idea.

Good old Joe and his female counterpart are inclined to be engaged to or even marry their first romantic interest. The fear of not being accepted by anyone else frequently leads them to foolish and impetuous behavior, including early marriage and/or promiscuity.

As an adult, good old Joe has a tendency to tell people only what he thinks they want to hear. He would never send an overcooked steak back to the kitchen. He lets others take his parking spot and doesn't object when a coworker takes credit for work he has done.

Speaking of parking lots, I like the story of the lady who was driving a big luxury automobile. She was headed for a spot in a big, crowded lot, and suddenly a young guy with a tiny sports car zipped right in front of her.

He hopped out, waved at her, and said, "When you're young and strong and athletic, you can do things like this."

The woman didn't say a word. She backed her car up, went charging right into his, and smashed it in the side. Then she backed up and hit it again. He came running back and said, "What on earth are you doing?"

She said, "You can do things like this when you're old and rich."

Don't misunderstand. If your self-image is so healthy that you truly view these incidents as minor and meaning nothing in your game plan for life, then your self-image is in excellent shape. However, if you acquiesce to gain acceptance, you're gaining everything but acceptance. The reason is simple: you're not presenting the real you. In fact, you're presenting a phony. Most people, including other phonies, don't like a phony.

Let's take another look at building a healthy self-image. I'm convinced that in addition to what we as individuals must do, we need to do something nationally about it. No snowflake ever blames itself for the blizzard, no raindrop ever blames itself for the flood, but each one of us has a responsibility to our country and to our society.

I want to be pragmatic in looking at one of the causes of poor self-image and what we can do about it. The news has been flooded with a fact that from the fifth grade on, girls are constantly harassed sexually by the boys. Something like 80 percent of them complained about having lewd remarks made at them, being patted and pinched, having obscene gestures made at them—a constant bombardment of that sort of thing. They commonly said, "This makes me feel dirty. It injures my self-esteem."

That's why I was so stunned when I read in the *Dallas Morning News* that you could not teach a sex education course in school and use the words *spirituality* or *soul* or *moral*. You cannot even say those words. One court recently ruled that you could not even use the word *abstinence* in a sex education course. They said that is a "religious" teaching.

I believe in things that work. If what they're doing would work, I'd tuck my tail between my legs and never say another word about it, but what they're teaching is not working.

Let me be very specific. In the schools where they teach sex education, 113 girls out of 1,000 who take the course become pregnant. According to a study by the organization Focus on the Family, in the schools where they teach moral values and abstinence, they have 3 pregnancies out of 1,000.

Now I'm a taxpayer. I have to support, as do you, the result of many of those pregnancies. Elayne Bennett, who is the wife of former education secretary and drug czar Bill Bennett, created a program in inner-city Washington called Best Friends. She teaches working together. She teaches abstinence. They teach moral values, and among students in the program there are very few if any pregnancies.

There's a fear of anything religious in our schools. The Constitution does not separate us from religion. It provides for freedom *of* religion, but not freedom *from* religion. Let me be very specific.

For over two hundred years in our schools, we taught biblical principles. The *New England Primer* was the original source. Do you know how they taught the alphabet? They would give you A, and they gave you a Bible verse. B, and they gave you a Bible verse. In 1963, that was changed, and it could no longer be done.

I'm not trying to get religion taught in school, but I am trying to get values taught in school. The reason is very simple. They work. According to *The Wall Street Journal*, 84 percent of all the people in America want values taught. In 1776, three million Americans produced Thomas Jefferson, George Washington, Benjamin Franklin, Alexander Hamilton, John Adams, James Monroe—you name them right across the board. In 1993, 250 million Americans produced—fill in the blanks.

What were they taught in 1776? Over 90 percent of it, according to the Thomas Jefferson Research Institute, was of a moral, ethical, and religious nature. As Ann Melvin of the *Dallas Morning News* said, "Something is wrong when we can teach a child to use a condom before recess but won't let them pray before lunch."

Psychiatrist Robert Coles of Harvard University says, "Many schoolteachers are afraid to bring up moral and spiritual questions for fear that they violate the Constitution. It's a tragedy intellectually as well as morally and spiritually. This might relate to the educational problems among some children. A large number of the schools' assumptions are materialistic and agnostic. There's a culture conflict between families and schools. That conflict may have some bearing on whether children learn and what they don't learn and how children behave in school."

Why am I so strong about this point? For years, we've had a course called "I Can." We don't teach religion, but we do teach honesty, character, integrity, hard work, enthusiasm, responsibility, and commitment. What is the result? Grades are better; attendance is up; drug use is down. Attitude is better—less violence, less vandalism.

Charlie Pfluger from Indianapolis came to one of our seminars on "I Can." He was the assistant principal at an inner city school in Indianapolis. He got so carried away with it he went back with more ideas and more excitement than he could use.

Charlie took a dollar coin, put it on a piece of cardboard, and cut it out. On one side, he put "PLA money," for *positive life attitude*. On the other side, it said "I can." They started giving the kids an I Can dollar every time they did something a little unusual. If they helped an old lady across the street, if they picked up trash on the school grounds without being told, if they erased the blackboard, if they graciously, courteously, and enthusiastically welcomed a new-comer to school, they would be given an I Can dollar. A student who accumulated $100 of these would be given a winner's T-shirt. There were 593 kids in this inner city school, and that was their last year there. Normally when students are about to leave school, nobody cares what happens to the school, but 587 of those kids won those I Can T-shirts.

Charlie said it got to be hilarious. They'd see a piece of paper blowing across the schoolyard, and there were nine kids out there running it down. The blackboards were cleaner than ever before in history. They'd help old ladies across the street when they didn't want to cross the street. When a newcomer would come to school, about seventy-five of the kids would welcome them.

You might say that's an expensive program until you hear the rest of the story: not one single act of violence, not one single act of vandalism, not one single drug arrest. Grades were better. Part of the curriculum required the kids to go home and thank their parents for something nice they did that day. For the first time, parents, teachers, and kids became a unit.

You know what they taught them in that "I Can" class? Respect, courtesy, enthusiasm, hard work, discipline—those are the values we're talking about.

For years and years, we have been intimidated. People say, never talk about religion or politics. I challenge you—tell me any two subjects that are more important than religion and politics. The fact that we haven't gotten involved in politics is the reason, ladies and gentlemen, we are in the turmoil that we are in, in our country today.

We have to put moral values back in our schools. Let me ask you, do you think honesty is a moral value? According to the Chamber of Commerce, folks, 50 to 60 percent of all businesses go bankrupt because of employee theft. And in recent years, 85 percent of all new jobs have been created by businesses of fifty people or less.

Now put those facts together. How many tens of thousands of people are out of work today because they were not taught moral values by their parents or the educational system? We need to look at that, and we need to look at it very carefully.

I believe that if you were to ask an individual who's been raped or mugged or wounded in a drive-by shooting, they'd say, "Man alive, I wish that person had been taught some moral values."

In one of many unfortunate cases, Donald Thomas, an African-American in Dallas, was killed by three skinheads who rode by and senselessly shot him, entirely because he was black. I'll guarantee you that his mother wishes they had been taught moral values in school.

Mary Crowley has been a friend and a hero of mine for many years. Many years ago, she said to me, "Zig, there comes a time in everybody's life where they encounter problems they cannot solve. That's when something greater than we are needs to take over."

If you've ever participated in AA or any of the twelve-step programs, you know that there are two keys. The first is to acknowledge that you cannot handle the problem. You need help from a higher power, God, as you understand him. The second key is that you stay sober by helping somebody else stay sober. Is that a moral value, accepting responsibility for your brother? I believe that it is.

Once I was in Atlanta doing a seminar. When it was over, a lady who was seated in the second row with her husband came up. She said, "Mr. Ziglar, I'm Janet McBarron. I wrote you a letter."

"Yes, Janet," I said. "It's an absolute delight to see you."

"I just wanted to elaborate on what I said in the letter," she said. "This is my husband, Duke. Like you, I weighed well over two hundred pounds for a number of years. As you can clearly see, I'm no longer overweight. Unlike you, I used to smoke two to three packs of cigarettes a day. I no longer smoke. Unlike you, I used to drink, and I'm embarrassed to say that on one or two occasions I drank too much. I no longer drink.

"I was a nurse," she continued, "I had been a nurse for eight years. I loved being a nurse, but, Mr. Ziglar, my self-image was absolutely at the rock bottom. It was down to zero. I started listening to you over and over."

That's why I keep saying repetition is the mother of learning. That makes it the father of action. That means it's the architect of accomplishment.

Janet went on: "I heard you quote Dr. Joyce Brothers, who said you cannot consistently perform in a manner which is inconsistent with the way you see yourself. I especially appreciated the fact that you kept emphasizing that life is tough, but when you're tough on yourself, life is going to be infinitely easier on you. I loved the fact that you kept saying, 'If you don't like who you are, and where you are, don't worry about it. You're not stuck with where you are. You can grow, you can change.'

"Mr. Ziglar, let me reintroduce myself. I'm Janet McBarron, MD. I worked my way through medical school as a full-time nurse. I'm one of five women in America who has their specialty in bariatrics—weight management, weight control."

I'm saying that the right input, her commitment, an awful lot of hard work, and a willingness to serve made a difference. Remember, we identify what people really want: they want to be happy; she and her husband are. Let me tell you one reason why.

As I've said earlier, others can give you pleasure, but you'll never be happy until you do something for somebody else. Today Janet McBarron is a published author. She has three clinics. Over five hundred thousand of her books have been sold. She has a heart for helping people. She says the most satisfaction she gets out of life is when she teaches the functionally illiterate how to read.

"Zig," she said, "you cannot describe the joy I get when I have a fifty- or sixty-year-old man or woman who is able, for the first time, to pick up a newspaper and read it, who can be in a strange neighborhood and not have to ask anybody, 'What street am I on?' Most of the older ones, for the first time in their lives, are able to read the Bible, and that seems to be what they center on."

You can be happy only when you do things for somebody else. Janet McBarron is a happy lady. She's a healthy lady. She's a prosperous lady. She's a secure lady. She has lots of friends. Her family relationships are magnificent. She has great peace of mind and tremendous hope for the future.

Let me say it again: if you don't like who you are, don't worry. You're not stuck with where you are. Janet McBarron read, listened, studied, took action, and did something for others.

I love what Helen Keller said in her autobiography. She records endless days of anticipation and despair, waiting for someone to draw her out. Then she records the day she first met her teacher, Anne Sullivan. This is what she wrote:

*I learned a great many new words that day. I
do not remember what they all were, but I do
know that* mother, father, sister, teacher *were
among them—words that were to make the world
blossom for me, "like Aaron's rod with flowers."
It would have been difficult to find a happier
child than I was as I lay in my bed at the close of
that eventful day and lived over the joys it had
brought me, and for the first time longed for a
new day to come.*

To build a healthy self-image, know that you're
not stuck where you are. You can grow, you can
change, and when your self-image is solid, you'll be
happy with your mate, your child, your job, and your
neighborhood. If you find fault with yourself, it's
easy to find fault with everything else.

I love what my friend and fellow speaker Mamie
McCullough says: "Every time you look at your hand,
you should concentrate on your thumb, and you
should look at your thumb and remember that you
really are thumb-body." Now that might be a silly
little way of doing it, but since I heard her say that,
every time I look at my thumb, I am reminded of it.

Now let me emphasize a point that is aimed primarily at the millions of Americans who at least
occasionally read their Bibles and go to church.
Some preachers in the past have tried to make you
feel guilty about being successful, and I want to deal
with that.

Take a sheet of paper and separate it into three vertical sections. At the top of the first column, write, "Be." At the top of the second write, "Do." At the top of the third write, "Have."

You will discover that everything you have is as a result of who you are and what you do. You have to be before you can do; you have to do before you can have. I challenge you to give me an exception to that.

Now, for you Bible readers, who are you? Look up John 1:12: "But as many as received him, to them gave he the power to become the sons of God."

What can you do? Look up Philippians 4:13: "I can do all things through Christ which strengtheneth me."

What can you have? Look up Romans 8:16-17: "We are the children of God: And if children, then heirs; heirs of God, and joint-heirs with Christ."

Now let me talk about a couple of words that give a lot of people a lot of trouble. One is *deserve*. I look up the word in the dictionary, and it says *to be worthy, fit, or suitable for some reward*. A laborer deserves his wages. Customers deserve service. And while we're on the subject, let me ask you, what's a reward? According to the dictionary, it's *to give in return*, either good or evil. Rewards and punishment presuppose moral agency and something voluntarily done, whether it's well or ill.

For 150 times in the Bible, we read about rewards. Look up Proverbs 24:20, Psalms 58:11, Matthew 5:12, and you will see a lot about rewards.

One last little thing for Bible believers. If you have a child, how does it make you feel when your child comes to you and says, "Mom or Dad, I'm a nothing, I'm nobody, I'm a loser. Let's face it. I am just a nothing"?

Doesn't that make you proud? Doesn't that get you excited? Do you say, "That's right, honey, and I'm glad that you've decided that you are where you are," or does it break your heart?

Do we have a right to criticize our Heavenly Father? When you say you're a nothing, you're saying, "God, let's face it, you just made a mistake." Folks, my Bible tells me God doesn't make mistakes. Ultimately it's going to work out.

THREE

Vote for You!

heard a story about the chairman of the board of a fast-food company who was making his rounds and checking up on how everything was going. He walked into one of his facilities about 10:45. Closing time was 11:00. He noticed no customers, nor was there anybody working.

The chairman looked through the opening at the door, and back in the kitchen he saw an employee smoking a cigarette. He about blew his stack. He walked around very briskly behind, and there was the manager, also smoking a cigarette.

The chairman proceeded to read them the riot act in no uncertain terms. Finally, when he got completely run down, the manager said, "And just who are you?"

The chairman of the board said, "I'm the chairman of the board of this corporation. What do you think about that?"

"I think ain't neither me nor you going to ever go any higher in this organization."

Sometimes you have to face reality, and I think he was right on the target on that one.

I love the story of the seventy-five-year-old gentleman. When somebody asked him, "Can you play the piano?" he said, "I don't know."

"What do you mean, you don't know?"

"I never tried."

Unfortunately, we often automatically say no when somebody asks us if we can do something, when in reality there's a chance that maybe we could. Now don't misunderstand. I'm certainly not trying to shortcut training, but can't you at least give something a try?

I love the self-image of the old fellow who was walking down the street, talking to himself. Somebody stopped him and said, "Why are you talking to yourself?"

"Two reasons," he said. "First of all, I like to talk to intelligent people. Second, I like to listen to intelligent people talk." Now I thought that made an awful lot of sense.

One important step in building a healthy self-image is to avoid certain things, like pornography. Psychologists say that three viewings of a pornographic film will have the same negative impact on your image as one action, and when you see mankind at his worst, you see a depreciation of your own value of yourself.

I'm going to make a strong statement, and don't squeal too loudly when I make it: I do not believe that you can be optimistic and morally sound and watch the daily or nightly soap operas. Here's the evidence I present.

Let me quote a weekly summation of the soap opera *All My Children.* If you want to have fun, cut out these weekly summations and get together as a family: the challenge is to read them with a straight face.

After Brian and Dixie make love for the first time as husband and wife, they argue about her plans to go to Napa Valley to find Tad. When Dixie catches up with Tad, she accuses him of being after Nola's money. Distraught, Tad runs to Nola's grave, where a vision of Nola tells him that Dixie needs him. He rushes to Dixie's side, and stops her from leaving with a kiss.

When Helen walks in on Adam and Gloria in the midst of an embrace, she calls Gloria a tramp. To appease Helen, Adam offers to pay for Walter's funeral. Helen makes Gloria's day by telling her that she is moving to Pine Valley.

When Taylor overhears Mimi tell Lucas that she can't sleep with him anymore because she has

chosen to be with Derek, Taylor runs to tell Derek.
Lucas then must do his best to convince Derek that
nothing ever happened.

You thought you had a bad week when you only broke one leg. Now think about what has just been described. In one week's time, one soap talks about two-timing, fornication, gold digging, promiscuity, distress, slander, appeasement, manipulation, lying, gossip, adultery, and bribery. How many of those are positive?

If you think that that was just a rare exception, let me cite one more, *Days of Our Lives*:

A videotape of the bogus Bo brutally beating Cash,
plus Cash's identification, causes Bo to turn in his
badge. Not satisfied, Lawrence blackmails Philip
into broadcasting the videotape in the hope of com-
pletely destroying Bo.

Upon learning that she doesn't have much lon-
ger to live, Vivian aborts her plot to kill Carly, but
she has another plan in mind. Marlena is taken
aback when Rebecca wearing only John's shirt
answers his door.

Although rejected, Austin still goes to bed with
Carrie for the Face of the Nineties contest, but
admits on Jennifer's show that he is available.
Victor finds out about Billie's forgery but lets it
slide because she is on cloud nine over her book
contract.

What have we discussed there? Resignation, false-hood, brutality, blackmail, revenge, forgery, a murder plot, rejection, and deceit. What do you think? Is that positive or negative?

The kids today say everybody is doing it, and they're partly right: everybody on television is doing it, but everybody in real life is *not* doing it. If TV sets this as the standard, more and more people will be doing it. I'm not only talking about fornication and adultery; I'm talking about revenge, violence, murder, thievery, and everything else.

You're what you are and where you are because of what's gone into your mind. You can change what you are and where you are by changing what goes into your mind.

We need to be repeatedly reminded that failure is an event; it's not a person. Churchill failed eighth-grade English three times and he had a speech impediment, but did that mean he could never be an outstanding writer and orator? I don't think anybody would make that statement. For a statesman and a leader, failure is a part of life.

Did you know that pitcher Nolan Ryan has probably lost more games than 99.9 percent of all of the people who will ever throw a baseball? We don't think of him as a failure, because he kept coming back and winning more.

Quarterback Roger Staubach has probably thrown more incomplete passes than 99.9 percent of the football players who will ever throw a ball. The same thing is true of Terry Bradshaw and Joe Montana, but do we think of them as failures? Not hardly. They kept on.

Did you know that George Washington only won two military victories in the War of Independence? The British kept pushing him back, but he was getting stronger and stronger.

Valley Forge, the toughest time of all, enabled us to win our independence. At Valley Forge, Baron von Steuben, the little Prussian officer, taught Washington's men discipline, close-order drill, and military attacks in formation, and they became toughened and more determined than ever. That's what brought about victory. It happens over and over that tough times develop us so we can produce good times.

Another step in building a healthy self-image: we need to know how to communicate. Communication is enormously important. Vocabulary is the key to communication, but confidence is what we build communication on.

I'm not necessarily talking about public speaking—being able to stand up and make a speech—rather, I am talking about effectively communicating with other people. Your communication skill and your listening skill are two of your most important assets. Listen. Learn to communicate.

Actually the best and fastest way to dramatically change the picture you have of yourself is to take a good course in public speaking. A lot of the colleges offer them. The Dale Carnegie people have an excellent one. Naturally our company has the best one, but at any rate, you need to develop that skill of communication. Most people credit somebody who can stand up and speak without collapsing with an intelligence they do not necessarily possess. Now don't let that get around, we want to keep that one very quiet, but that is a matter of record.

Learn how to stand up and address a group of people. What it will do for your image is absolutely remarkable. Let me give you two or three fast steps you can take.

Number one is, if you're afraid of talking to a group, don't talk to a group. When I speak, I speak to people individually. I've never met a person in my life that I wasn't willing to talk to, and chances are, you haven't either. Talk to them one at a time.

If somebody is out in the audience who is an old sourpuss, don't think that you have to win them over and make friends with them. Instead, seek out the person that is responsive and friendly, and talk to that person. Get your support and encouragement from them.

Have you ever heard of Alben W. Barkley? He was a longstanding senator, and vice president of the United States under Harry S Truman. After he left office as vice president, he ran for the Senate again and won. In a speech he gave on April 30, 1956, he said he was willing to sit with the other freshman senators, despite his long years in the Senate before he was vice president. He ended with an allusion to

Psalm 84:10, saying, "I'm glad to sit on the back row, for I would rather be a servant in the House of the Lord than to sit in the seats of the mighty." He then collapsed onstage and died of a heart attack.

I mention Barkley because he was one of very few people to have given their lives making a public speech. The odds of your dying while speaking in public are infinitesimally small. Folks, it's safe; it really is. More people get killed bathing than they do speaking in public. So step up with confidence.

I will give you another little tip. You could lead an old Mississippi mule across a stage, and he'd walk right across. He wouldn't be the least bit concerned about the audience, but if you led a thoroughbred, I guarantee you that he'd be all over the place. So if you get a little nervous when you stand up to speak, be grateful that you're a thoroughbred and not a mule. It will do a lot for your self-image.

Another tip for enhancing your self-image: recognize that nobody really look likes those TV models and those glamour pictures. A failure to realize that creates problems among a whole lot of people. Be fair to yourself.

Make the right choice; that will have a marvelous impact on your self-image. It's safe to say that most problems are caused by a poor self-image. We retreat, we don't go forward, we don't do the things we really are capable of doing. We sell ourselves short.

That's the reason I keep going back to the growth process. The Japanese raise bonsai trees. Bonsai take years and years to cultivate and develop. It is an art. They are absolutely beautiful. The bonsai tree, which can be any one of a number of species, is anywhere from twelve to twenty-two inches tall. When the little tree pokes its head above the soil, they extract it, they tie off some of the feeder roots and tap roots, they carefully shape it, and they watch it grow.

There's a tree out in California call the General Sherman; it's a giant sequoia. The General Sherman is nearly 300 feet tall. It's wide enough that you could drive two automobiles through it side by side. Engineers have estimated that if they were to cut it down and saw it up into lumber, they could build thirty-five five-room houses.

Now the interesting thing is this: the bonsai tree and the General Sherman, at one time, were approximately the same size. Each weighed less than one-three thousandths of an ounce when they were seeds, but the bonsai tree had its growth stymied and stunted. The General Sherman was nourished by the richness of the California soil, by the sunshine, and by the rain. As a result, it grew to a forest giant.

Neither the bonsai tree nor the General Sherman had a choice, but you have a choice. You can grow. Tomorrow is a brand-new day. Yesterday is gone. Make friends with yesterday, focus on what you can do today, and plan and prepare for tomorrow. That's when life takes on new meaning, and accomplishments grow. That's when we have the best chance of being happy, healthy, reasonably prosperous, and

secure, and of having friends, good family relationships, and peace of mind.

Now I'm going to share my own story with you,
because for most of you, my story is your story. With
three exceptions, you and I have walked in the same
pair of shoes.

The first difference, for some of you, is that I have
never lost a mate or a child through death or divorce.
I do not know how it would feel to have suffered that
loss. I can say to you, "I know how you feel," but the
reality is, try as I might, I really cannot, because how
could I know the depth of your love and your feeling
for your loved one?

The second possible difference is that I have had
somebody who loved me all of my life. It's true that
my dad died when I was five years old. Times were
very tough, the six of us were too young to work,
money was short, and a lot of other things, but my
mother always had plenty of time for loving me and
all of my brothers and sisters. My older brothers and
sisters also loved me. I have also been lucky to have a
mate who has always loved me. I can safely say that
she loves me more today than she ever has, and I love
her more today than I ever have. I have four children.
I'm safe in saying that each one of them loves me. I'm
doubly fortunate in that my three sons-in-law and
my daughter-in-law also love me. I have been greatly
blessed in that area.

The third possible reason that we might not have
been walking in the same pair of shoes is this: I've

always been healthy. I've never had any emotional problems. I have never had any serious physical problems. If you have, again, I can say to you, "I know how you feel," but the reality is, I cannot.

As for being discouraged, being broke, being uncertain about what tomorrow's going to bring, or not having a clue about what I was going to be doing or how I could handle any number of situations, I have walked in all of those pairs of shoes.

So in many ways, our story is the same. I was raised in the little town of Yazoo City, Mississippi, during the Depression. We survived after my dad's death. He died on Thursday; my baby sister died the following Tuesday. We had five milk cows and a big garden.

I was milking cows before I was eight years old, and I know that some of my readers are city slickers, and you don't know a whole lot about cows. So let me tell you something about cows: they don't *give* milk. Now I don't know what you can do with that information, but there it is. You use it as you see fit.

As a youngster, I worked in the garden and did all the other things that my brothers and sisters did. I was very small for my age, and in those days we didn't have poor self-images; it was called low self-esteem or inferiority complexes. One manifestation of a poor self-image is that you're impatient. You cannot solve problems. You have to get on with it. For example, when I disagreed with somebody, if we could not solve it in ten seconds or less, I would rear back and bust them one. I never discriminated about whether they were bigger or smaller, whether they were black or white or anything in between.

A Mexican boy broke me of that habit. I have never been as glad in my life as I was to see Miss Street, my third-grade teacher, come to the rescue, but in all fairness to me, I scared that poor guy half to death. He thought he'd killed me. I learned a lesson there.

I went to work in a grocery store when I was just nine years old. I worked every afternoon after school and all day Saturday. I was a teller. I'm not trying to impress you with the title; it just meant I told people to move while I swept. I was not in management.

In those days I made 20 cents for working from 3:20 in the afternoon until 7:00 at night. I earned 75 cents from working from 7:00 in the morning until 11:30 on Saturday night. I earned a grand total of $1.75 a week working all those hours. I know what it is to need a dollar and want a dollar, but I learned a lot of things.

For example, my boss, Mr. Anderson, was a former schoolteacher, and when I would drop a grammatical boo-boo, he would always correct me. He became a surrogate father. He had a big farm, and every Wednesday afternoon he used to take me out there and let me watch him as he talked with the laborers.

Mr. Anderson showed me an awful lot of things by example. I remember vividly one day when a man came in with some kind of a promotional idea. As a ten-year-old, I sat there listening to it, and boy, it sure sounded good to me. My boss never even considered it. When the guy left, I said, "Mr. Anderson, why didn't you go along with that idea?"

He said, "Well, you know, I don't know a whole lot about what he was talking about, but I learned a long time ago that you can't make a good deal with a bad guy. If his word is not his bond, you better walk away." I found that to be true all of my life: you can't make a good deal with a bad guy.

When I was twelve years old, I added a paper route to my everyday activities. On Tuesday and Friday nights, I delivered the *Yazoo Herald*. One night a week, I collected for the *Herald*. I was a busy guy.

When I entered the twelfth grade, I moved next door. The man who'd been running the butcher shop there in the Yazoo City Piggly Wiggly store was named Walton Haining, and he wanted me to come next door and work with him in the butcher shop. I worked with him that last year.

Then I got into the Naval Air Corps. Incidentally, there's nothing that's ever happened to me that's given me as much confidence and boosted my image as much as getting in, because it was the tail end of World War II, and very few were making it. I'd always considered myself below average, and yet for some reason, I wanted to fly those airplanes so badly that I applied. When I made it, you cannot begin to know what that did to my image.

I was to report for duty on July 1, 1944. The night before I was to leave, Mr. Haining took me aside, and he said, "Zig, the war is winding down. I know you'll be back in a couple of years. I'd like for you to work for me when you get back."

"Mr. Haining, I don't think I'd be interested in that."

"Why not?"

"There's just no money in a grocery store."

He pulled out his tax returns from the year before. He said, "Let me show you something, Zig. Last year, after all taxes, I earned $5,117 for the year." In this age, that doesn't sound like a whole lot of money, but he was earning $100 a week, and let me tell you what you could do in 1944. You could buy three pounds of good bacon for 27 cents. You could buy a twenty-five-pound sack of good flour for 55 cents. I bought a little jacket for 87 cents. I'm here to tell you that in 1944, $100 a week was a ton of money.

Mr. Haining said, "If you will come back and work for me for two years, I'll teach you everything you need to know about running a market. I will help you get your own location and another store. I'll help you get your credit established, and you can own your own business."

Man alive, I couldn't wait. The next day I was so excited. I was going to go off to war, and I was going to get that thing over with. I was going to come back to work for Mr. Haining for two years. I was going to get my own market, and I was going to earn me $5,117 in a single year. I was motivated.

At 9:06 p.m. on September 15, 1944, I walked into the YWCA on State Street in Jackson, Mississippi, for the first and only time. Standing over by the nickelodeon was the prettiest little auburn-haired girl I'd ever seen in my life. Man alive, did I ever fall for her.

I went over to her, and with an enormous amount of originality, I said, "Hi." With equal originality, she responded, "Hi." The courtship was on. Now I have to confess to you that when I first saw her, I wanted to walk over, grab her, hug her, and start kissing on her right then and there. That's what I wanted to do, but if I had, I would have skipped too many steps, and I can guarantee you, she would not have become my wife.

I make this point for this reason: in life, there are a lot of steps, folks, and you have to take them. It is not an overnight thing, and if you've been going down one path for many years, don't expect to instantly reverse the whole process, but one step at a time, you can do it. You can eat an elephant a bite at a time. You can accomplish some amazing things if you build the right foundation and take the right steps.

I got in the Navy and met that little redhead, and then my plans changed. In 1946, I was going to the University of South Carolina. Uncle Sam had sent me up there as part of the training program. When they discharged me, I decided to go back up there, and in November 1946, we got married.

I was selling sandwiches around the dormitories at night to finance the marriage and my education. I conceived the idea and bought a little grocery cart. I'd load up the milk and the sandwiches and the coffee cakes, and I'd go around selling them.

I did extremely well during the regular school year, but when summertime came, the enrollment dropped to less than one-third of what it had been (no air-conditioned dormitories). The guys and girls started going out at night to get their little snacks, and I had to look for something else to do financially.

The redhead saw an ad in the paper for a $10,000-a-year salesman. I went down and applied for the job. It was in direct sales, selling cookware on a person-to-person basis on commission. I had to buy my samples. But they did not believe I could sell. They turned me down.

It took me two full months to convince them that they should at least give me a chance. They finally did. They said, "We'll put you through the week of training, and if at the end of the training we think you can sell, we will give you the contract," but they wouldn't even tell me what the commission was or anything else. They really did not think I could do it.

At the end of the week, I guess they figured they had nothing to lose, so they gave me the contract. For the next two and a half years, all I did was prove they had been right to start with. That doesn't mean I didn't sell a lot, because I did: I sold my furniture; I sold my car. That's awfully close to the truth. I had my lights turned out; I got there just in time for them to turn them back on. I've had my telephone disconnected. Again, fortunately, I happened to be stopping by, and I had just enough money so they could reconnect that telephone.

I've gone down the grocery line and miscalculated, so I had to put a loaf of bread back, and that's when bread was a dime a loaf. I bought my gasoline 50 cents' worth at a time.

I never will forget the day I had 50 cents in my pocket and my old 1940 model Studebaker quit running. I stopped in front of a mechanic's little shop under a shade tree, and I told him, "Sir, my car quit running. Let me tell you before you even raise the hood, I have 50 cents. That's all I have to my name, but I sure need my car running. If you would just look at it." Well, he looked it, and it was the points. He reset them, and I was off.

When my first daughter was born, the hospital bill was $64. I didn't have $64. I had to get out and make two sales before I could even get my own daughter out of the hospital. I'm here to tell you I know what it is to be broke.

This went on for two and a half years. One time, I was doing so miserably, I asked Bill Cranford, my sales manager, "Go with me. Find out what I'm doing. Help me. I have to make some sales." He went with me on a call. When it was over, I said, "Bill, what do you think?"

"Well, Zig, let me ask you. What are you selling?"

"Bill, you know what I'm selling."

"Yeah, I know, but don't you think you should have told that lady?"

"Bill, it wasn't that bad."

"Come on," he said. "Let's go to the training room."

We went to the training room, and he recorded my talk. It was a nineteen-minute presentation. I said "uh" 187 times. Later on, I became the fastest drawl in the West, so you really can change.

The other people were putting on group demonstrations where they bought the food, paid a hostess a premium to sponsor the demonstration, and sold to the prospects.

I wanted to do that, but I had three basic problems.

Number one, I didn't have the money to buy the groceries or the premium. Number two, I did not know the first thing about cooking, and number three, I had never seen a demonstration, but with the confidence that generally goes with ignorance, I figured I could do it.

I heard of a Mrs. B. C. Moore, who lived at 2210 High Street on the corner of Colonial Drive. I can see that home as clearly in my mind today as I could that day. It was a white, two-story frame house, no air conditioning, no insulation, and it was August. It was brutally hot. She had a set of our cookware, but she didn't like it because she didn't know how to use it.

I said, "Mrs. Moore, I'll make a deal with you. I will teach you how to use that set of cookware if you will invite in two prospects and if you will buy the food for the demonstration."

She said, "It's a deal." She invited Mr. and Mrs. Clarence Spence, her sister and brother-in-law, who were living with her while their home was being built, and Dr. and Mrs. M. P. Gates. He was a dentist who had a set of the cookware. They didn't like it either, because they didn't know how to use it.

I put on the demonstration. Apparently it was at least satisfactory. I didn't burn anything. When it was over, Mrs. Spence made a five-minute speech. She went into great detail about how tough times were, how they were building a house, how they were in debt, and how they were struggling to make ends meet.

My heart got heavier and heavier as she was talking, but she said, "You know, I'm always in debt. We're always broke. If I don't go ahead and get this nice, heavy set of cookware right now, I never will be able to get it. I'll take it."

Mrs. Gates took her cue from Mrs. Spence. She too made a five-minute speech. I don't know whether they were trying to impress me or their husbands or their hostess. She made the same speech, but it ended up the same way: she said, "I'll take it."

Now, folks, let me repaint the scene. Here I was so broke that if it only cost 50 cents to go around the world, I couldn't have gotten out of sight. There were two ladies with their money in their hot little hands, saying, "I'll take it." What would you have done under those circumstances?

Guess what Old Zig did. Scout's honor, I looked at my watch, and I said, "Ladies, I'd like to sell you that set of cookware, but I can't. I have another appointment, and I'm running late now. I'm going to have to go and see them."

With two ladies with their money in their hot little hands, saying, "I'll take it," I said, "Oh, no, you won't. I have something important to do," and out of there I scooted. When I got to the other appointment, obviously the prospects were not there.

Here's my question. On your dumbest, greenest day, if you have sense enough to get out of a telephone booth without written directions on the side, would you ever have done such a thing as that? What I'm trying to say is, friend, there is hope for you.

My whole world changed one day. I went to an all-day training session in Charlotte, North Carolina. I lived in Lancaster, South Carolina, which was about thirty-eight miles south. I spent the day but didn't learn a thing.

I got back home that evening. I had a demonstration; I conducted it and got in about 11:30 that night. Our daughter kept us up most of the rest of the night. At 5:30 the next morning, the alarm clock sounded to get me up to go to the second day of the training school. By force of habit, I rolled out of bed. We were living in a little three-room apartment above a grocery store. I cracked the Venetian blinds, looked out, and said, "Ziglar, anybody with bat brains won't get out there amidst all of that ice and snow, driving a little old Crosley automobile without a heater. Man, don't be ridiculous."

I did what any intelligent person would do: I got back in bed. But as I lay there, the words of my mother came back to me (again, here's that repetition, which is so important). My mother preached to me a thousand sermons: "When a task is one begun, you leave it not until it's done," and "Be a matter great or small, you do it well or not at all." She said that your word is your bond, and she also said, "If your word is not worth anything, then nothing about you or what you have is worth anything at all."

When I had taken the job, I had agreed that I would be at every sales meeting and every training session. Although I had done nothing in the business in two and a half years, not only had I never missed a meeting, I had never even been late for one. That early input rolled me out of bed, and I went to the meeting. That's where my whole life changed.

A man named P. C. Merrell was there. Mr. Merrell was my hero. He had set all of the records with that company and written all of its training programs. I still don't remember what I learned in the session itself, but when it was over, he took me aside. He said, "Zig, I want to talk to you privately."

I was thrilled to death that Mr. P.C. Merrell, my hero, was willing to spend a few minutes just with me. There were twenty-one other people there he could have talked to. He chose me.

The conversation lasted probably less than two minutes. By design or by happenstance—I don't know which it was—he got me in a corner and said, "Zig, I've been watching you for the last two and a half years, and I have never seen such a waste." Now that will get your attention.

I said, "Mr. Merrell, what do you mean?"

"Zig, I believe you could be a great one. I believe you could go all the way to the top. I believe you could become a national champion. I believe, Zig, that if you really recognized your own ability and went to work on a regular schedule, someday you could be an executive in this company if you chose to do so."

Please understand. He was talking to a little guy from a little town who was going to struggle all of his life. I never thought I'd live in the slums, but neither did I honestly think I'd have more than one suit of clothes. Here's a man saying, "You could be an executive. You could be a national champion. You could be a great one."

"Mr. Merrell, do you really believe that?"

"Zig, I know it."

My picture of myself changed dramatically. There's an old and true statement: a lot of people have gone a lot further than they thought they could because somebody else thought they could.

Now I want to emphasize two points. First of all, Mr. Merrell was a man of unquestioned integrity. I knew he was speaking truth; I knew that was the way he felt. Had I thought for one moment that he was just telling me that so I'd sell more cookware and he would look good, it would have had zero impact. But knowing him as I did and knowing his reputation, when he said, "You could be a great one," I believed him.

Now let me emphasize the second point. When he said, "Go to work on a schedule," it was enormously important. At that point, I knew how to get prospects. I knew how to make appointments. I knew how to conduct demonstrations and handle objections, and I knew the sales closings.

The salesman was ready, but the man was not ready. Until you get the man ready, the salesman is not going to be ready. Until you get the person ready, the teacher is not going to be ready. You have to be before you can do. I had already been trained in the skills and techniques, and now the confidence that goes with a healthier self-image was my own.

When I left the meeting that day, I was floating on cloud nine. That little Crosley automobile without a heater never touched the ground on the way back.

Had the three couples at the demonstration that evening been even half smart, they would have opened by saying, "OK, Zig, we know you're going to be the national champion this year. Don't worry about the demonstration. Just give us something to eat, man, and we'll go ahead and buy." They never had a chance.

I had not learned anything about selling, but I learned a whole lot about me. When my image changed, everything about me had changed.

I finished that year as the number-two salesman in America out of over seven thousand. I had the best promotion that company had to offer. The next year I was their highest-paid manager in the United States. Three years later, I became the youngest divisional supervisor in the sixty-six-year history of that company.

Ever since then, I've never given a talk without praying, "Lord, make me a P.C. Merrell in the life of the people who are there."

I travel a lot. I get to meet a lot of people. I seldom get to know anyone, and I'm the loser as a result. I wish I could. I wish I could meet and come to know every person who sits in my audience, picks up one of my books, listens to one of my tapes. I wish that I could get to know that person on a personal basis, but of course I know that is impossible.

If I could, I would look you straight in the eye, and I would say to you, "You were born to win. Out of the twelve billion people that have walked the face of this earth, there has never been another one like you. You're rare. You're different. You are special. You are unique. You're fearfully and wonderfully made. You were born to win, but in order to be that winner, you have to plan to win; you have to prepare to win. Then, and only then, can you legitimately expect to win."

I don't know if you voted in the last election; I hope you did. I think that we as citizens need to participate in every election locally, statewide, and nationally. If we don't, we have no right to complain about anything that is going on. We have abdicated the right to gripe if we've not accepted the responsibility of doing something about it. But I'm going to ask you now to cast a vote of an entirely different nature. I'm going to ask you to vote for *you*.

Here's the process. Imagine that you can step directly into the polling booth of your own mind. Imagine that you reach up and pull the draperies shut, because this is a very private affair. As you make this particular vote, here you are in the voting booth, and there are a lot of levers there.

One of those levers has a name on it that is pure gold. It's bigger than any of the others. It has your 'name on it. You reach up, and you grab that lever with your name on it. You pull it down, excited, motivated, enthusiastic, and you vote for you. When you do, you'll discover that long ago God had already voted for you. The eternal arithmetic clearly says that you plus God equals enough.

FOUR

Stop Kicking
the Cat

A lot of people have difficulty with relationships. In this chapter, I'm going to share some ideas that will help you to build better, winning relationships.

A lot of people start off well. It's like the lady who was talking to a friend; she said, "You know, when we were first married, we got along wonderfully well, but then we left the church."

I love the story of an executive called Mr. B. He called a meeting one day and told all of his people, "Now, folks, we've been doing well, but we can do a lot better than we've been doing in the past. I have to confess that much of the difficulty has been lying with me. I've not been the leader that I'm capable of being. I've not set a good example, but from here on in, I'm going to get here early. I'm going to stay late. I'm going to take short coffee breaks and short lunch breaks. I'm going to be the example, and I encourage everybody to follow through, because we can be so good in this company. We can grow so fast. We can do so much."

It was quite an inspiring speech, and Mr. B really intended to follow through, but you know how folks are. They forget those speeches after a little while. A couple of weeks later, he was out at the country club having lunch, and he forgot all about the time. Suddenly he looked at his watch and realized he was due back to the office in four minutes.

Mr. B. hopped up, made a mad dash to the parking lot, and went off doing ninety miles an hour down the freeway. The long arm of the law entered the picture and gave him a ticket.

Mr. B. was absolutely furious. When he got back to the office, he was steaming. He said, "The very idea of this man out there worrying about somebody breaking the speed limit a little! He ought to be looking for robbers and murderers and rapists and people who are really breaking the law. Leave us peaceful, tax-paying citizens alone."

Mr. B. walked into the office, and you know what we've always done: when somebody catches us with our hand in the cookie jar, we tend to say, "Look there" to divert the attention. He walked in, he called for his sales manager, and in a loud voice he said, "Come into the office. I want to talk to you."

The sales manager came in. Mr. B. said, "I want you to tell me about the Armstrong account. I want to know what's been happening with it. You've been fooling with that deal for three weeks. You should have closed it a dozen times. Bring me up to date."

The sales manager said, "Mr. B., I don't know what happened. I had it; I thought I had it. I thought it was all signed, sealed, and delivered, but at the last minute it just came unglued, and I lost the deal."

If you think Mr. B. was upset before, you should have seen him now. He hit the ceiling. He said, "You've been my sales manager for sixteen years. I've been depending on you to bring business in. Here we had the chance to really have a big breakthrough, and what do you do? You blow it. Let me tell you something, friend. Just because you've been here for sixteen years does not mean you have a lifetime contract. You're going to replace that business, or I'm going to replace you."

Mr. B. was upset, but if you think he was upset, you should have seen the sales manager. He went storming out of there and said, "This is ridiculous. For sixteen years, I've been running this company and brought in all of the business. If it hadn't been for me, it'd have gone bankrupt years ago. Now, just because I fouled up one deal—it could have happened to anybody—he blames me."

The sales manager was really upset. He called his secretary and said, "I want to know where you are on that Hilliard account."

"Well," she said, "I've been working on three or four other things at the same time, and you said they took precedence."

"Look, don't give me any lousy excuses. I want that account taken care of. I want those letters gotten out that I've given to you, and I want to know if you got them out."

"No. I've been busy on the other projects."

"Just because you've been here for eight years doesn't mean you have a lifetime contract. If you can't do better on these things, I'm telling you right now, I'm going to get somebody who can."

The sales manager was really upset, but if you think he was upset, you should have seen that secretary. She went storming out of there, saying, "This is ridiculous. I've been running this company for eight years. If it hadn't been for me, it'd have gone bankrupt years ago. Now, just because I can't do three things at once, he jumps all over me. This is not fair. Who does he think he's kidding, firing me?"

The secretary walked out to the switchboard operator and said, "Look, I have a half dozen letters. I want you to get them out. I know this is normally not your job, but you don't do anything anyhow but sit out here and occasionally answer the telephone. I'm telling you right now that if you can't get them out, I'll get somebody who can."

The secretary was really upset, but if you think she was upset, you should have seen that switchboard operator. She said, "That's ridiculous. I've been here over ten years. As a matter of fact, I'm the glue that holds this company together. If it weren't for me, we'd have gone out of business years ago. Now here they are, not doing a thing in the back but gossiping, talking, and drinking coffee. I'm worked to death out here, and then they load something on me and say, 'If you don't do it, we're going to fire you.'"

The switchboard operator got the letters out, but when she got home, she was furious. She walked in, and the first thing she saw was her twelve-year-old son lying on the floor, watching television. The second thing she saw was a big rip right across the seat of his britches.

She said, "Son, how many times have I told you? When you come home from school, you're supposed to put your play clothes on. Mother has a hard enough time as it is supporting you and sending you through school. Now because you've been disobedient, go upstairs right now. There's going to be no supper for you tonight and no television for the next three weeks."

That operator was upset, but if you think she was upset, you should have seen that little boy. He hopped up and said, "That's ridiculous. I was doing stuff for my mother. She didn't give me a chance to explain. It was an accident. It could have happened to anybody. It wasn't my fault." About that time, his tomcat walked right in front of him, which was a mistake—a bad one.

The boy kicked the tomcat. He said, "You get out of here. You've probably been up to no good yourself."

Now let me ask you a couple of questions. Wouldn't it have been much better if Mr. B. had just gone directly from the country club to the operator's house and kicked that cat himself?

Whose cat have you been kicking? Let me ask you another question. Has anybody been kicking your cat?

Have you ever been waiting at the go light for the right color to come along, and just as the light changes, all of a sudden there's a screaming horn right behind you? It's an instant that elapses between the time the light changes and the horn behind you sounds. You hear that horn, you turn around and say, "Can't you see we have other people in front of us? I'll be going in just—." Can you understand that it has nothing to do with you? Somebody has been kicking that dude's cat all day long.

Have you ever gone into a restaurant to get a cup of coffee? You sit there, and you sit there, and finally you hold up your hand and say, "Ma'am, could you get me a cup of coffee?"

She says, "Can't you see I'm busy? I'll get to you just as quick as I can."

How do you respond? Do you say, "Well, you don't have to bite my head off?" or can you understand it has nothing whatever to do with you? Somebody had been kicking her cat all day long.

Have you had a marvelous day when everything went your way? You close the big account, you've gotten a lot of proposals out. You're on a roll; it looks as if it's going to be the best month of your entire life.

At home, you walk in whistling and singing and call out to your wife, "How are you doing, honey?"

"You know how I'm doing," she says, "and if you'd been here putting up with what I've been putting up with all day long, you wouldn't be feeling so good yourself."

Can you understand that it's not about you? Somebody has been kicking her cat all day long.

We're emotional people. When we deal with people, can we get in a situation where we do not let those emotions control us and how we feel?

Of course, much of this is aimed at myself, because, you see, all of us need to be reminded sometime. Let me remind you that everybody wants to be happy and healthy, they want to be reasonably prosperous, they want to be secure. They want to have friends, they want to have peace of mind. They want to have good family relationships, and they want to have hope.

Those are the things most people want in life. Much of that depends upon your job or profession, and much of that job or profession depends upon your relationships with other people. Getting that job, getting that promotion, and keeping that job are very often determined by the relationships you have established. People hire you and keep you on the payroll because of your productivity, but also because they like you.

What can we do to make certain that those relationships are solidly built? Let me give you ten commandments of human relations. They're not originals by any stretch of the imagination. You'll recognize virtually all of them.

1. You speak to people. Now that's elementary, isn't it?

2. You smile at people. It takes seventy-two muscles to frown and only fourteen to smile, and a smile is the first thing you notice about others.

3. You call people by name. You've heard it a thousand times.

4. You're friendly and helpful to people.

5. You need to be cordial. Speak and act as if everything you do is a genuine pleasure.

6. Be genuinely interested in other people. You can like almost anybody if you really try.

7. Be generous with your praise and very careful with criticism.

8. Be considerate of the feelings of others.

9. Be alert to giving service. What counts most in life is what we do for others.

10. Add a good sense of humor.

The best thing to do behind a person's back is to pat it. If you meet somebody with a chip on the shoulder, the best way to get it off is to let them take a bow. This is very elementary, yet it is enormously important.

People want to be right, they want to be appreciated, and they want to be understood. The Department of Labor says that 46 percent of people quit their jobs because they did not feel appreciated. These ten commandments will help solve some of that.

Although we want to be always right, none of us can be right every time in everything that we do. But we can let people know we understand how they feel. When we say no to someone, we can cushion it by adding, "I appreciate your position."

All of us are emotional. Everybody says, "I make logical decisions." In a pig's eye you do. Sometimes you may deal with the facts, but when you really get right down to it, it's the heart that has the most influence.

Have you seen the movie *E.T. the Extra-Terrestrial?* If you have, did you cry when that little dude kicked out? Very likely you did. Now here's an alien from outer space, not even a person, and it's on the screen, so you know it's imagination, and yet you sat there crying like a baby.

Are we logical? No way. People don't act logically, they act emotionally, and the best way to get along with them is to understand them and try to get on their side of the fence. When we do that, it improves those relationships.

Although we need to be sensitive to the way the other person feels, we don't want to go overboard. We certainly don't want to let paranoia set in.

I was reading about a youngster who enrolled in a new school; I believe he was in the second grade. His mother, being a very sensitive lady, started querying him about the makeup of the class. She asked, "Son, are there any minorities there?"

"Yes," he said, "there is one black person there, an African-American."

"Do you play with this person?"

"Absolutely not."

The mother proceeded to give the boy a lecture on racism, and then she asked, "Now are you going to be more cooperative and play with this person?"

"No, ma'am."

"Why not?"

"Mom, she's a girl."

What I'm really saying is get information, get the facts, and then you can act in a better way.

We need to be more sensitive. We need to be more understanding. Yet the least sensitive people on earth never recognize this fact. They're obnoxious. On many occasions, they'll defend themselves by saying, "That's just the way I am"—so you supposedly ought to accept them as they are and let them go ahead and be boorish.

I saw a cartoon one-liner that says it all. A personnel manager to a young woman: "Sexist? Don't be ridiculous. We employ plenty of dames."

Yet it's true that some people are tough to deal with. They're just obnoxious. They have barracuda personalities. We need to understand that, but we also need to understand something about their nature.

My friend and mentor Fred Smith says, "When others are mean and nasty and rude to you, that in most cases, they do not want to hurt you. They're that way because they are hurting."

In many ways, every obnoxious act is a cry for help: "Understand me. Help me to get through this." The Center for Creative Research did a study, conducted by Michael Lombardo, Morgan McCall, and Ann Morrison, and here's what they learned.

Most successful executives had, at one time or another, had a boss who was impossible, but they learned to deal with that impossible boss and get along with him or her. They acknowledged that it was the impossible boss that made it possible for them to develop tolerance and growth, overcome obstacles, and obtain their positions of success. In addition, the difficult bosses helped these executives form their own best management techniques and procedures. They had seen an individual who was tough to deal with, and they determined they were going to do it a whole lot better. The experience helped them acquire the patience to deal with conflicts constructively. It turned out to be a good teacher. They avoided destroying that relationship; instead they built the relationship, learned from it, and benefited from it.

What can we learn from our relationships with our bosses? According to these behavioral psychologists, never forget that he or she is your boss. It is your job to do the work the way the boss wants it done. You're paid to do your job in a way that makes the boss's job easier. You're there to remove obstacles for the boss, not to be an obstacle. Again, the responsibility begins with us. Management will judge you by how well you get along with the boss, and that judgment will affect your progress. Working with or around a rotten boss teaches you how to set priorities, neutralize potentially explosive situations, and choose your moments.

I've mentioned John Foppe. Because he was born without arms, John has to solve more problems creatively every day than you and I have to solve in a month's time. For this reason, he quickly developed a great deal of maturity and is able to understand how other people feel. For this reason, he is far more successful than almost any other twenty-two-year-old I have seen in my life.

Don't try to change the boss. There's only one person in the world that you can change, and that's you. When you change, you can more effectively deal with the other person. Remember, don't let the way the other person treats you affect or determine the way you treat them.

Most of us know the story of Helen Keller. She was born a perfectly normal little girl, but very early she was afflicted with a terrible disease that took away her sight and her hearing.

As a result, her family pitied, pampered, and spoiled her. She became incorrigible—a little girl that nobody could get along with. Although you felt sorry for the fact that she was in that condition, she was a spoiled kid.

The first day that Anne Sullivan was brought into the household to work with Helen Keller, Helen picked up food and threw it on her, screaming or trying to scream with what pitiful voice there was there.

Anne Sullivan simply looked at her and said, "Little girl, you can act as you want to, you can be as mean and as obnoxious as you choose to be, but I don't see you in the same way you see yourself. I believe you were put here for a purpose. I believe inside of you there is enormous potential. I'm going to love you, and I'm going to treat you in such a way that this potential is going to be brought out."

We know Helen Keller's story. Anne Sullivan was the individual whom God used to make that story a reality. Anybody that can treat people that way really would be remarkable, but the potential of the human being is astronomical. We need to be careful about the way we judge others versus the way we judge ourselves.

I read this recently and was impressed with it:

When the other person blows up, he's nasty; when you do it, it's righteous indignation. When he's set in his ways, he's obstinate; when you are, you're just being firm. When he doesn't like your friends, he's prejudiced; when you don't like him, you're simply showing good judgment of human nature. When he tries to be accommodating, he's polishing the apple; when you do it, you're using tact.

When he takes time to do things, he's dead slow; when you take ages, you're deliberate. When he picks flaws, he's picky; when you do, you're discriminating. When he reads the riot act, he's vicious and insensitive; when you do it, you're just being honest for his own good.

Isn't it amazing how we set those double standards? Rare indeed is the person who can weigh the faults of others without putting his own thumb on the scales.

When we hire young people and they stay with us over a period of time, and as we watch our children grow, we seem to forget that they're growing, developing, maturing, and becoming more capable all the time. I was amused again by a little clipping out of *Reader's Digest.*

My mother's always treated me like her baby, no matter what my age. After turning thirty, I purchased a computer and learned to use it. Thinking I'd impress her with my skill and maturity, I sent her a well-written letter, complete with computer graphics, borders, and an elaborate typeface. I phoned to ask what she thought of the letter.

"It's lovely dear," she replied. "I have it hanging on the refrigerator for all the neighbors to see."

Let me plead guilty. One Saturday afternoon several years ago, I was coming back from an out-of-town trip. I stopped by the office to pick up my mail, and as I did so, Lisa Carpenter, who worked with us at that time, was walking out the door. I said, "Lisa, what are you doing here on Saturday afternoon?"

"I just came by to pick up the supplies I need for the training session I'm conducting this afternoon."

All of a sudden it hit me like a ton of bricks. We had hired Lisa as a part-timer when she was still in school. She was a neat, pleasant student and a very bright worker, but with all my travels, I had not spent a lot of time talking with Lisa. I had completely forgotten that she was one of the most capable speakers and staff members we had. I had not kept pace with her growth in my mind.

It's one of the most serious mistakes we make in management. It's one reason that a lot of people go and seek greener pastures elsewhere: they say, "I cannot get recognition here and respect for what I'm doing."

Let me stress here that you treat people as you see them, and the way you treat them determines your relationship.

Years ago, a young lady went to work for the Hilton hotel chain. She was doing quite well. She got word that Mr. Hilton himself was going to be a guest in the hotel the next day. She had never seen him. She asked the other clerks, "Have you seen Mr. Hilton?" They'd not seen him either, but knowing that he was going to be a guest, she got all uptight. She said, "Oh, boy. I hope that I don't foul up if I'm the one who checks him in."

The next evening, she got a call from Mr. Hilton. He said, "When I checked in this afternoon, you were so professional, you were so gracious, you were so friendly. I am delighted to have you as a member of the staff."

She never knew that he had checked in. She had been treating every male with the thought, "Maybe this is Mr. Hilton."

Why don't we treat everybody like VIPs? Would it make a difference in the relationships we have with them? I think we all know the answer to that.

Your happiness is determined more by the success of your relationships than by any other single thing. If you're not getting along well with the people who are important to you, you're one miserable human being.

Your relationships will have a direct bearing on your effectiveness on the job. They'll have a direct bearing on your health. They'll have a direct bearing on your happiness. They'll have a direct bearing on your hope, your security, and everything else. If your relationships are not going well, you start finding fault with everything you do.

As we've already learned, the way you see your business is going to play a major role in how effective you are in that business. In other words, your business is not out there; your business is right in here, between your ears.

The way you see yourself has a direct bearing on how effective you are in your relationships, because if you can get along with you, then it's infinitely easier to get along with others. By now, you should be comfortable with the way you see yourself so you can easily adjust and see others properly. That's important because, again, the way you see them determines the way you treat them, and the way you treat them determines their performance.

Nowhere is discipline more important than it is in the way we deal with people. When you meet somebody who's rude and nasty and obnoxious, the inclination is strong to bite back at them, but the future that you have in a lot of companies is determined by that relationship. According to executive recruiters, seven people out of ten who lose their jobs do so because they do not have the right kind of relationships. There are personality conflicts.

Basically, we live in a self-centered, "I want to be me," "I want to be free" society. "Let it all hang out. Let me express myself." A lot of songs have the refrain, "I want to be free." Yet if you take the train off the tracks, it's free, but it can't go anywhere. If you take the steering wheel out of the automobile, it's under the direction and control of no one, but it can't move.

Think about it in this light. The sailor only has freedom of the seas when he or she has become an absolute slave to the compass. Until you are absolutely obedient to the compass, you have to stay within sight of shore. Once you're obedient to that compass, you can go anywhere in the world the boat you're on will take you.

When we become so disciplined that we no longer utter everything that's on our mind, when we control our voice, we have a better opportunity to get ahead in life. Do you respond to the way people treat you, or do you react?

I love the story of the Berlin Wall. When it was erected, obviously with a lot of construction, they had a lot of garbage and trash. Before the wall was sealed, the East Germans took a lot of that trash and hauled it over to West Berlin.

The West Berliners got pretty unhappy about that. They decided they would load up a dozen truckloads of garbage and haul it back, but wiser heads prevailed. Instead, they got together a huge truckload of food, medicine, and blankets, and they sent it back across with a little note, "Each gives what each has to give."

What do we return? What is in it for us, you might ask? Let me tell you what happens when we adopt the kind of attitudes I'm talking about. According to author Norman Shidle, a group becomes a team when each member is sure enough of themselves and their contributions that they can praise the skill, abilities, and contributions of others. Again, it's back to the self-image. When you're comfortable with yourself, fear and prejudice go right out the window.

I think one of the most moving newspaper photos that I've ever seen was taken at the end of the 1992 Army-Navy game. Army had won that particular game. This particular photo shows Brian Ellis, the Navy quarterback, who had just thrown a last desperation pass, but it had been intercepted. The photo shows him on his knees; his head is bowed. It also shows an Army defensive back, Cadet Gaylord Green, who was an African-American, standing there with his helmet in his hands, his face against the helmet of his fallen adversary. He was simply saying to him, "We just played a tough game, but underneath we're on the same team. We're brothers." A classic example of what happens when prejudice is eliminated.

Now, folks, you know today in our society, service is the buzzword. You hear it everywhere you go: service, service, service. That's what we have to do, and service involves relationships. Henry Ford said this, "A business absolutely devoted to service will have only one thing to worry about, and that's profits. They will be unbelievably, embarrassingly large."

The reality is that there are a lot of people who only give lip service to service. Now why is that? Because you can't have service without a servant, and for whatever reason, in our society today, a lot of people think that if you're going to be a servant, you have to be servile. Nothing could be further from the truth. As a matter of fact, two thousand years ago, the carpenter from Galilee said, "He who would be the greatest among you must become the servant of all."

In dealing with a lot of top executives around the country, I have observed that they really do have a servant's heart. They want to help other people progress and go ahead in their own lives. As Henry Miller said, "Render a service if you would succeed. This is the supreme law of life. Be among the great servers, the benefactors. It is the only path to success. Give, and it shall be given unto you. Make society your debtor, and you may find your place among the immortals."

Nobel Prize-winning physicist Clinton Davisson said, "If you want to become the greatest in your field, no matter what it may be, equip yourself to render greater service than anyone else."

Albert Schweitzer said, "I don't know what your destiny will be, but one thing I know, the only ones among you who will be really happy are those who have sought and found how to serve."

Let me emphasize that the words you use are important. The titles, the names, the way you address people are very important as well.

When our third daughter was born (our son didn't come until ten years later), we knew perfectly well that we were going to have trouble with our second daughter. How did we know?

Very simple. Our friends and relatives had all told us, and I'm here to tell you that they were absolutely right. It started the day we got home with the new baby from the hospital. As you know, the neighbors and relatives all come in. They make a beeline to the bassinet, and you know how people always talk to new babies: "Coochie, coochie, coochie. Oh, isn't she cute? Look at the way she holds her head up."

They spent a lot of time there. Our oldest daughter would be standing right there, and the neighbor would say, "Oh, I know that you're going to love this little sister. You're such a big girl. You're going to be an awful lot of help to mommy. Can I take your baby sister home with me?" They really put it on thick for the new baby and the oldest one, but what about that oddball stuck in the middle? "Well, hi there"—that was about the extent of it.

Cindy, our middle daughter, became a griper, a whiner, and a complainer. As she would do things, old Dad would say over and over, "Why can't Cindy be like everybody else? Why can't she be like Julie (our baby), or Susan (the oldest girl)? Why does she have to cry and whine all the time? Just one time, if that young 'un could be a happy little girl, I would be so happy."

I have to confess I handled this with sheer genius, if I do say so myself. I gave her a nickname. It was Tadpole. When I introduced my children, I'd say, "This is Tadpole." Every time somebody would come over, I would say, "I want to introduce you to Tadpole, the happy girl in our family, the one who's always laughing and smiling and having a wonderful time. Aren't you, baby?"

She'd look up and give me that little two-front-teeth-missing grin and say, "Yes, sir."

One day, after about a month, one of the neighbors came over and I said, "I want to introduce you to our happy little girl. Tell them what your name is, baby."

"Oh, Daddy, I've changed my name."

"What's your name now, baby?"

"I'm the happy tadpole."

Family is so important. So is the language we use on them and the way we treat them. Again, you treat people as you see them, and the way you treat them has a direct bearing on their performance. Can you take negatives away and make them positive? Most of the time, you can.

I remember Barry Tacker from Bay City, Texas. I addressed the school down there in relation to our "I Can" course. They told me about Barry Tacker, the disciplinarian. Now I don't know how many states have disciplinarians in their schools, but at this time, that particular school did. Do you think that most kids get excited when they get a chance to see the disciplinarian? It brought forth fear and trembling.

But when Barry Tacker became the disciplinarian, he changed the rules of the game and instituted a new policy there. On the first day, a teacher said to one of the youngsters, "OK, you need to go see Mr. Tacker."

The kid said, "What did I do?"

"I don't know, but apparently it's pretty serious. You need to go see Mr. Tacker, and you need to see him right now."

The youngster walked down with fear and trembling, and said, "Mr. Tacker, I don't know what anybody told you, but I'm not the one who did it. I plead innocent."

Mr. Tacker said, "Well, I have several eyewitnesses that you are the guilty party, but before I did anything at all about it, I wanted to confront you directly to see if it really did happen in both cases. If not, then I'll apologize and send you back to the classroom. One of your classmates said that they saw you warmly greeting a new student in school yesterday and telling them how glad you were that they're in the school. Now do you plead guilty or innocent?"

"Well, yes," said the kid, "as a matter of fact, I did."

"Not only that, but you were seen picking up some trash on the schoolyard and helping a senior citizen across the street. Now did you or did you not—"

"Oh, yes, I did it. I did it."

"Does your mom know what you're up to every day of your life?"

"I don't know."

"Well, she needs to know. I'm going to give you this note. I want you to take it home and get your mom to sign it. It says that you have pled guilty to warmly greeting a new student in school. You pled guilty to picking up trash. You pled guilty to helping a senior citizen across the street. I want this signed and brought back tomorrow."

Now let me ask you: do you believe that approach is likely to get good results? What do you think they thought about Mr. Tacker? What do you think the kids thought about the school?

Let me tell you one of the facts of life: the behavior which is recognized and rewarded will be repeated, whether it's negative or positive.

When a four-year-old holds his or her parents hostage in the grocery store, kicking and screaming and demanding a toy or some special food, and mom and dad are coerced into giving in, you can absolutely count on it that on the next go-around, exactly the same thing is going to happen again. Behavior, whether it's good, bad, or indifferent, if it's recognized and rewarded, will be repeated.

The words you use do make a difference. They're very important. Somebody once said that one picture was worth ten thousand words, but that individual had obviously never read the Declaration of Independence, the Bill of Rights, or the Twenty-third Psalm. They're all words, but they paint such vivid pictures, and they give so much information.

What words are important? The most important thing you can ever say to a child is, "I love you." You may say, "I demonstrate my love by providing them with a home and food and education and everything they need." Even so, let me tell you, the kids want to hear you say, "I love you."

The second most important thing you can say to them is, "I made a mistake. Please forgive me." A lot of parents believe that that would undermine their authority, but nothing can be further from the truth. What you're really saying is, "I'm wiser and have better judgment than I did an hour earlier or yesterday." Nothing pleases a child more than to know that you are willing, and you're secure enough in your role, to say, "I made a mistake."

"I appreciate what you said or did," are very important words. So are "You were a big help." "That's a great idea." "Thanks for your input." "What is your opinion?" "You are important." Thank you." The most important word is *you*. The least important word is *me*.

Remember, people want to be right, and they want to be understood. Remember too that the input in their minds is going to determine their output in life.

As should be clear by now, I'm a great believer in putting forward the good, the clean, the pure, the powerful, and the positive, but please don't misunderstand. When somebody is consistently doing and saying the wrong thing, you need to have one-on-one visits with them and explain the bounds in which they can operate.

I'm talking as much about attitude as about anything else. What is the tone of your voice? When you were growing up, did your parents say to you, "Watch the tone of your voice, young man or woman"? Have you ever said that to your kids? It's not what you say, it's the way you say it.

One of the most fascinating stories I've ever heard involves the Babemba Tribe in South Africa. They're a very gentle and peaceful tribe. When a member of their tribe does something that is anti-social, they have the whole village get together and put that individual on trial. They have a big pow-wow or meeting in the center of the village, with the individual on trial in front of them. They start with the very youngest person in the tribe who's old enough to express themselves. The child will say to them, "Do you remember the night you held me on your lap, and we were around the campfire, all of us talking and eating, and you shared your food with me?"

A somewhat older child would say, "Do you remember that you were the first one who taught me how to bait a hook and how to set a trap for some game?"

Another one, still a little older, might step up and say, "Don't you remember, you're the one who told me how to find the trails in the forest?"

Every member of the tribe is called on to make some comment about this individual. It must be true, and it must be positive. They have to tell them of all of the good things they have done, and the message that keeps coming in is: "I can't believe a man or a person with all of these good qualities would do this antisocial thing."

The records show that there's almost never a second time where the individual has behaved in an antisocial way. "As you sow, so also shall you reap." Garbage in, garbage out. Put the good stuff in, you get the good stuff out.

How do you build winning relationships? You put a lot of the good things in, starting with a genuine interest in the other person.

FIVE

The True Power of Words

One fellow married a lady that was several years older than he was. She was extraordinarily wealthy, and for about five years, they had a wonderful time together. They traveled the world, lived in a huge home with swimming pools and butlers, and always drove luxury cars. They went to all the best places to eat.

Then the wife died. A few months later, a friend said to the husband, "I know you lost your wife, but she left you in pretty good shape, didn't she?"

The old boy kind of smiled, and he said, "Well, yes, she did, but you know, sometimes I miss her so much I think I'd give $1,000 just to have her back."

Many people don't quite understand how to be appreciative of other people. In this chapter, we are going to give particular emphasis to the fact that you can have everything in life you want if you will help enough other people get what they want. This is not a tactic. It is a philosophy. Walmart founder Sam Walton put it this way: "I discovered that by enriching others, I enriched myself." This applies in our personal life, family life, and business life.

Again, let's identify what everybody wants. Everybody wants to be happy, to be healthy, to be at least reasonably prosperous and secure, to have friends, to have peace of mind. They want to have good family relationships, and they want to have hope that the future is going to be even better.

That's what everybody wants in life, but what about work? What do people want there? As somebody once said, perception is the cruelest form of reality. A study was reported in *USA Today* about what managers thought their workers wanted and what the workers themselves wanted. These were quite different.

The managers thought that the personnel wanted, number one, good wages; number two, they wanted job security; number three, they wanted promotions in the future. That's what the managers thought the workers wanted.

When the researchers asked the workers, they got an entirely different perspective. The first thing they wanted was interesting work. Number two was appreciation for the work they had done, and number three, they wanted a feeling of being in on things.

Let's start by assuming that we know what the employer wants: productivity, quality merchandise, and the loyalty of the employees; they also want a profit. Isn't that basically what every owner of every business wants?

Let's also assume that the employer makes certain, or works to make certain, that the employee has interesting work, and that the employer shows appreciation for the work done. As I've already pointed out, according to the U.S. Department of Labor, 46 percent of the people who quit their job do so because they do not feel appreciated.

One study by James Howard, a consultant to our company, asked people, "What does your boss or immediate supervisor say when you've finished an assignment?" and 92 percent said, "Nothing." How does that make you feel? Does that motivate you?

Let me ask you: do you believe that if the boss provides interesting work, shows appreciation, and gives employees the feeling of being in on things, that would make them happy?

Do you believe that your attitude and your happiness have anything at all to do with your health? Do you believe that if employees are happy and healthy, they're going to do better work and consequently have a chance to get a raise and go up the economic scale? In other words, their chances of prosperity increase.

Does it give the workers a greater feeling of security to know that they're doing their job and are being appreciated? Do you believe that having these things going for them would help their attitude? Would they be more outgoing and friendly, and as a result would they have more friends?

Does all of this contribute to the employee's peace of mind? If you have good things going on at the job, does it make sense that you will have a more relaxed attitude and will probably have better relationships at home? In other words, when you go home from work, if the boss has said, "Good job," instead of "You lazy rascal," it does make a difference, doesn't it? That improves family relationships, and if you put all these things together, that gives them hope. As I've already noted, people want to have hope. Studies done at UCLA discovered that if you have hope, love, and faith, it strengthens your immune system.

Now the employer has provided what the employee wants. The employee gets the benefit, but what about the boss? He's thinking, "I'm in this deal to make a profit. That's the reason I opened my business." With all of these things going for them, does it make sense that employee's productivity would go up?

If you have a job where the boss is giving you everything you want, would you want to keep that job? I don't think anybody would ever say, "I don't want a job like that."

What does the boss want? Quality work. If employees are getting all of these other things, aren't they more likely to say, "My company" or "our company" instead of "the company" or "that company"? Isn't that the kind of employee that will be loyal to the employer?

According to *Fortune* magazine, Merck & Company was voted as the number-one employer in America—the most desirable place to work—for seven years in a row. The magazine listed ten criteria, and Merck placed first in eight out of ten.

Why would Merck be so interested in employee satisfaction? Very simple. They discovered that replacing a valued, skilled, trained employee cost them the equivalent of one and one half years of salary. So economically it behooves Merck to work to keep their employees happy.

What does all of that do to the bottom line? Do you believe that these advantages enhance the company's chances of making a profit?

You see, it is absolutely true that you can have everything in life you want if you will just help enough other people get what they want.

I love what the late business counselor Robert Updegraff said along these lines: "In terms of downright happiness, the returns per minute from giving are far greater than the returns for getting." When we're givers, things do happen.

In the business world, the number-one quality that owners and managers are looking for is the ability of each employee to get along with others. If you have one person who is a sour apple, who is disgruntled, not carrying their part of the load, and creating problems, that individual will do tremendous damage by bringing productivity down. As you well know, generally part of the company does not go out of business; they're all in it together.

Let me tell you one of my favorite stories about being oriented toward other people. Two of Britain's greatest prime ministers were William Gladstone and Benjamin Disraeli, who lived in the nineteenth century. Although both Gladstone and Disraeli were tremendously effective as prime ministers, they were totally different personalities.

A story is told about a titled English woman who was at a banquet one day with one of those prime ministers and with the other one a week or two later. In those days, it was the custom to pair up men and women alternately at the dinner table, and etiquette demanded that the man and the woman talk to each other.

The day after the lady had dinner next to Mr. Gladstone, somebody asked her, "What did you think about Mr. Gladstone?"

She said, "When I listened and talked with him, I became convinced that he had to be one of the brightest, wittiest, best-informed, most knowledgeable human beings I have ever seen in my life. It was absolutely astonishing, the amount of wisdom and knowledge that this individual had."

After the lady had sat next to Disraeli, the same person asked, "What did you think about Mr. Disraeli?"

She said, "After talking with Mr. Disraeli, I became absolutely convinced that I was one of the wittiest, brightest, most pleasant and knowledgeable persons on this earth."

Had these men been running against each other, which one do you think this lady would have voted for? No question about it, is there? Which one would she have followed the furthest? Which one did she think was the smartest? Disraeli, of course, because he had put her in front of himself. When you get wrapped up in yourself, as some people have an inclination to do, you really do make a very small package.

Several years ago, I injured my right knee bowling. One of my friends, who is not overly bright, made some reference to my age. I know he wasn't very bright, because if he'd thought about it for long, he would have realized that the other knee was exactly the same age as the injured one, and nothing was wrong with it, so obviously age has nothing to do with it.

Anyhow, I was scheduled to speak the next night. There was a large group of people, about three thousand. I walked out on the platform, and as I did, I was noticeably limping. I could almost hear and feel the audience saying, "Look at that. Old Zig is kind of crippled, but I know he's going to give it his best shot. Bless his heart. I know he's going to do it." I could just feel it coming from the audience.

They put that microphone around my neck, and I don't know about the therapeutic value of a microphone around your neck as it relates to sore knees, but when they did, my knee quit hurting. For the next sixty minutes, I was up and down, around and about, stooping, squatting, shouting, whooping, doing all of the things I normally do, and I'm telling you, the thing went over well.

When I got through, I took the microphone off, stepped down off the platform, and hit the deck. My knee collapsed. Why did it not bother me at all for sixty minutes and then suddenly go awry?

I think the answer is very simple. For sixty minutes, I was wrapped up in serving an audience. Although I did not do this consciously, when I finished I apparently thought, "Boy, I'm glad that's over. Now, Ziglar, you can think about yourself," and boom. That's when I hit the deck.

One of my favorite stories is about the great industrialist Andrew Carnegie, who had forty-three millionaires working for him. This was a hundred years ago, when a millionaire was much richer than a millionaire today. A reporter asked, "Mr. Carnegie, how on earth did you hire forty-three millionaires?"

Carnegie smiled and said, "When I hired them, none of them were millionaires."

"What did you do to develop them to the degree that they became so valuable to you that you could pay them enough money to become millionaires?"

Carnegie taught us a tremendous lesson with his answer: "You develop people in exactly the same way you mine gold. When you go into a gold mine, you expect to move tons and tons of dirt to find an ounce of gold, but you don't go in there looking for the dirt. You go in there looking for the gold."

You really do find what you look for. So many people have been told so many times what they cannot do. They've been so heavily criticized that they really do not know what they can do. They don't even know what they want, because they do not know what's available for them. They can understand that somebody else can get it, but for poor little old me, there ain't no way.

People who build winning relationships are what I call good finders. When we first moved to Dallas in 1968, I met one of the most fascinating men I ever met. His name was Walter Hailey, and he was in the insurance business. In those days, virtually all insurance was whole life; there wasn't much term insurance being sold. A million-dollar producer was a pretty good producer. A two-million-dollar a year producer was outstanding. Walter devised a method of marketing through mammoth grocery warehouses that enabled his representatives to sell $10 million, even $15 million worth of life insurance each year.

When I met Mr. Hailey, he said, "Zig, I want to take you over and let you see one of these mammoth warehouses. You won't believe how many groceries they can put under one roof." He was absolutely right. I didn't know there was that much food in the world.

We walked in the front door, and there was a huge switchboard and a lady who was in charge of it. There were others, but he walked up to her and said,

"Excuse me, Zig, just for a moment." He said, "Ma'am, I just wanted to tell you, you're absolutely the greatest on this switchboard I have ever seen. You make me feel that you've been waiting for me to call, and it makes me feel so good. I just wanted to tell you how much I appreciate you."

She said, "Why, thank you, Mr. Hailey."

We walked on down one of the corridors and got to a little office, and he said, "Just a minute, Zig. Let's step in here for a second." We stepped inside, and there was a gentleman. Mr. Hailey stepped up, and he said, "My name is Walter Hailey. I have not met you, but I have been watching your results. You know, we haven't had a problem in this department since you took over. I just want you to know how much I appreciate you."

The man said, "Mr. Hailey, I do the best I can."

"Well, you're certainly doing a good job. Keep it up."

We walked upstairs, into Mr. Hailey's outer office, and there was his secretary. He walked over and said, "Zig, shake hands with the greatest secretary who ever sat behind a desk. I believe, and my wife believes, that she hung the moon, and I'm just asking you right now, don't you ever take it down. I like it where it is."

She said, "Mr. Hailey, you're mighty sweet to say that. Thank you very much."

We walked in his office, and there sat one of his agents. Walter said, "Zig, shake hands with the greatest insurance salesman to ever put on a pair of shoes."

The guy said, "Oh, Walter, you're just always full of that sort of thing, but I really like it. Keep it up."

The whole trip took less than ten minutes. Let me emphasize something: you never say something to somebody that you would not say behind their back, whether it is good or bad. If you would not give a person that kind of a compliment behind their back, then you're talking about flattery. If it's sincere, however, then a compliment is verbal sunshine.

That whole extra trip took less than ten minutes. But do you believe that as a result of those ten minutes, those four people were more productive that day than they would normally be? It's better to have one person working *with* you than it is to have three people working *for* you. When you form a team, you can get more done. That's a winning relationship. That really is what it's all about—being thoughtful of the people you're with and around.

A few years ago, I was speaking at an insurance company banquet in Dallas. Two vice presidents and I were seated at the head table. I was in the center. There were three other executives with the company over on the other side.

When the lady who was waiting on us brought us the salad, I smiled and said, "Thank you." A few minutes later, she poured the coffee, and I said, "Thank you." A few minutes later, she served the entrée, and I said, "You know, I'm astonished that you're doing this so quickly, and yet you do not seem to be in a hurry. You're so pleasant to the people around you."

She said, "Thank you very much. I appreciate you saying that."

When the two vice presidents' coffee was poured, their salad served, and their entrée delivered, they didn't even grunt. They didn't say anything.

Finally came dessert time. The dessert was a chocolate sundae. It was a scoop of ice cream with some chocolate syrup poured on it. I exaggerate not one iota when I tell you that those two vice presidents got a scoop of ice cream about the size of a golf ball. My scoop of ice cream was bigger than my fist, and the chocolate syrup was running all down the sides.

"Zig, you obviously know this lady," said the executives.

"No, I don't know her, but I sure know a lot about her."

"How do you know that?"

"I recognized right away that she was a human being, and there isn't a human being alive who does not genuinely appreciate a courteous, enthusiastic individual who appreciates the effort that they were rendering."

Now I wasn't doing all that to get more ice cream. That's not the deal. I don't eat much ice cream (I found out a few years ago my body actually retains ice cream), but again, it simply says that you can have everything in life you want if you'll just help enough other people get what they want.

The story is told of a fellow who was given a tour of heaven and hell so he could choose where he wanted to end up.

He went to hell first, and there they had a banquet table set out that was absolutely unbelievable. It was a block long, had every delicacy the world has to offer—all the fresh fruits and vegetables and meats and sweets, the whole schmear. The people seated there at that table were half starved. No smiles on their faces, no laughter, no gaiety, nothing.

Then the guy was taken to heaven, where they had exactly the same menu—every imaginable thing—but here the people were laughing and joking, they were well-nourished, they were singing and having a marvelous time. It was a wonderful place to be. The man said, "I don't understand. You have exactly the same menu, but in one place they're happy, and in another place they're miserable. What's the difference?"

The guide said, "Had you looked carefully, you would have noticed that a three-foot fork and a three-foot knife are attached to the arms of each person. In hell, each person was trying to feed themselves and could not, but in heaven, they simply were feeding the person directly across from them."

I believe that's more than a parable. I believe that's life. In this life of ours, we live with an awful of people. Our ability to get along with them to a large degree determines just how happy we're going to be.

If you'll check the records, you'll discover that regardless of how everything else is going, if you're not getting along well with the people who are important to you, you're not a very happy camper. If you look in the other direction, I don't care how badly things are going in every area of your life, if you're really getting along well with the people who are important to you, overall you're basically a pretty happy individual. Psychologist Les Carter has said that 100 percent of all of his counseling has to do with relationship problems, either between husband and wife, brother and sister, parent and child, neighbors, or whatever.

I believe that winning relationships are built on trust, respect, and genuine interest in the other person. From time to time, you may be deceived if you trust too much, but you're going to live in torment if you do not trust enough.

How do you build winning relationships? You learn from chess players and athletes. In chess, all of the parts that you play with are out right in front of you. In championship matches, frequently the chess master will get up, go around—this is permissible, of course—and look at the scene from his opponent's side, because sometimes they see it a little differently. I believe that's a good idea. Try to see it from the other person's perspective.

In athletics, your objective is to analyze your opponent, find out where they're weak, and exploit that weakness. In football, boxing, tennis, basketball, or any other sport, you probe to find out where your opponent is weak, and you exploit it.

Similarly, in life, in selling, in medicine, in management, in education, you determine where your opponent—that is, your prospect or your client or your student—is weak. But here you strengthen that weakness. If you find out their needs and help them meet them, you're going to be doing your job in the most effective way.

One way of building winning relationships is to eliminate gossip. I heard a little fellow say one time, "I hate to spread gossip, but I don't know what else you can do with it."

I overheard these two people talking, and one of them said, "Tell me more."

The other one said, "I can't. I've already told you more than I heard." Unfortunately, there seems to be too much truth in that.

When somebody says to me, "Did you hear about—?" I say, "First of all, let me get you to do one thing. If you don't want me to repeat this and give my source, I encourage you not to tell me, because I forget who tells me what and whether it's a secret or not. It's too much of a burden for me to try remember what I can tell and what I can't tell. I talk a whole lot anyhow, so if you don't want me to tell, simply do not tell me."

People don't like gossips. Have you ever noticed that? When people don't like you, they'll hurt you if they can. If they can't hurt you, they won't help you. If they have to help you, they won't hope for you. If they won't hope for you, even if you achieve the victory, it is a hollow one. Author and pastor Dr. John Maxwell said that, and I believe there's much truth in it.

Here's what we read out of *The Wall Street Journal*: "The snake that poisons everybody, topples governments, breaks marriages, ruins careers, busts reputations, causes heartaches, nightmares, and indigestion, spawns suspicion, generates grief, and dispatches innocent people to cry on their pillows—even its name hisses. It's called *gossip*."

I love this also: "I'm an office mystery. I'm never seen, but I'm everywhere. I'm always on the job and often forecast important events. I make and unmake morals, reputations, and cooperation, but I'm seldom blamed for my mistakes. I have no responsibilities, and I am one of the most powerful molders of opinion. I add humor and anger to the office, and I pass with the speed of sound. I am basic in human nature, and you must accept me. I grow right behind you. I am the office grapevine." How true.

If you want to build winning relationships, you need to remember that the mic is always open and the lights are always on. Often when celebrities are questioned about something they said, they reply, "I didn't know that was for public consumption," or "I didn't know the microphone was on," which is pretty ridiculous.

Several years ago I was speaking at a trade school up in Tulsa, Oklahoma. The media somehow or other had learned that I was going to be there. As I was speaking, roughly one-third of the kids were sitting there, all ears, on the edge of their seats. They were really lapping it up. They were having a wonderful time. Roughly one-third of the students sitting there were reading newspapers or magazines, and roughly a third were leaning back, acting as if they were going to sleep.

When the television camera came in, they started at the very back of the room. The bright light on the front of the camera was on, and they were videotaping the kids in that audience. The camera operators walked straight down, came up on the side of the platform, and came behind me, shooting me talking to the students.

In ten seconds flat, I saw the most amazing transformation in an audience I have ever seen in my life. The papers disappeared; the magazines disappeared; everybody sat up straight. They started straightening their hair.

"Now, kids," I said, "I want to observe something for you. A few minutes ago, many of you could care less about what I had to say. Possibly you could still care less, but all of a sudden, you're very concerned about your image. Well, your image is not a thing in the world but the way you really are. Sooner or later, it's going to show itself.

"You can fool some of the people all of the time and all of the people some of the time, as the saying goes. At work you can fool the boss, you can even fool the people around you, but as employers, you will never fool the people below you. They get to see you, warts and all. They get to see the good part and the bad part.

"Remember that the lights are always on and the mic is always open. If you keep that in mind, you'll be able to go further in life."

Above all things, we need to make sure that our hearts and our attitudes are right. I like the story of this young woman who was talking with her mother. The daughter's friend Linda showed up in the long driveway, and the daughter said, "You know, Linda is so slender. I just hate her."

The mother said, "Come on. You know perfectly well that there's something you can do about that."

The daughter said, "There sure is. Linda, I'm sure glad to see you. I've been saving you a big, ol' piece of chocolate cake."

That's not exactly the approach I had in mind.

How important are relationships? God issued two commandments on which he hung all the law and the prophets: one, love God; two, love your neighbor as yourself. Albert Einstein put it this way: "*Love thy neighbor as thyself* is like a natural law, almost like a physical part of the universe."

How important are words? On a weekend several years ago, the redhead and I were at a little resort area. We were scheduled to play golf. We were to tee off at around 1:30. As often happens on holiday weekends, things get backed up and delayed.

When we got there, I knew we'd be at least thirty minutes late. We were putting and piddling around until tee-off time started. Finally, there was one foursome in front of us, and the redhead and I were standing there waiting for them. This young Adonis was on the tee box. He was six feet, four inches tall, weighed about 240 pounds, and had a forty-eight-inch chest and a thirty-one-inch waist. He was the kind of guy you could instantly dislike. He had muscles in places where I don't even have places.

This young man stepped up to the tee and teed his ball up. He took his driver, laid it down and picked it up, and he laid it down and picked it up again. He would get ready, and then he would look up.

I turned to the redhead and said, "That guy's not a golfer, that's for sure."

"How do you know?"

"Come on, sweetheart. I've been playing golf a long time. I've seen a lot of golfers, and I can tell you that dude is not a golfer."

Finally, after what seemed like forever, the young man drew the club back, and he busted that sucker 240 or 250 yards right down the middle. So much for my golf expertise. He walked over to his cart, put his club in his bag, and walked straight back to me.

He said, "Mr. Ziglar, I heard what you said. . . . when you spoke in our community about two years ago. It completely changed my life. I want you to know it's an honor for me to be on the same golf course with you."

I don't need to tell you that I felt about two inches tall, and the thought occurred to me right then and there as I silently asked for forgiveness, "What would my impact have been on him had he heard what I said then?"

One man I admire a great deal is Rabbi Daniel Lapin. As I frequently say, I never say or write something until I've checked it out psychologically, theologically, and physiologically, because we are physical, mental, and spiritual beings. Unless we put all these aspects together, we risk being in error. I do a lot of talking with Rabbi Lapin about the theological aspects of what I discuss.

Rabbi Lapin has this to say in his publication *Thought Tools*: "If we listen as others are maligned, in spite of our disinclination to believe what we hear, our relationship with a vilified individual is forever altered." In other words, we are involuntarily influenced by everything we hear.

Harmless gossip does not exist. Listening to gossip can even leave us feeling dissatisfied with our spouse, children, employees, friends, or life in general. Uttering gossip usually leaves us feeling less worthy. Words penetrate to our souls and cannot be erased or ignored.

In Leviticus 19:14, it says: "Thou shalt not curse the deaf." But if a deaf man can't hear, what's the damage? The damage is done to the individual who utters those words. Acid destroys the vessel which contains it.

"Overcome your inhibitions," Rabbi Lapin says about talking to yourself. "Speak passionately to yourself. Prepare speeches by actually saying them out loud. A winning mindset is the consequence of hearing words that penetrate right to the core of personality. If we truly wish to believe something, we should tell it ourselves audibly rather than think it silently."

Our language should be so clean and friendly that we could give our talkative parrot to the priest or minister. Many times today we hear people use what they perceive to be adult language. I'm also guilty of using an enormous amount of adult language—words like *honesty*, *responsibility*, *optimism*, *discipline*, and *commitment*. These too are words of adult language: *decisive*, *dedicated*, *competent*, *dependable*, *consistent*, *punctual*.

I don't know where they ever got the idea that filthy and vulgar words were adult. Any four-bit psychologist will tell you that using them is a mark of insecure, immature individuals who do not know how to express themselves any other way; they resort to cheap language hoping that they can get somebody's attention. They do get their attention, but it is not favorable attention.

I also use a tremendous number of four-letter words—words like *hope*, *care*, *love*, *good*, *team*, *warm*, *free*, *able*, *kind*, *nice*, *wise*, *hero*, and *help*. Of course, one of my favorite four-letter words is the word *Jean*. That just happens to be the name of the redhead I'm married to. When I say that four-letter word, I guarantee you, it brings a smile to my face. Four-letter words can be enormously helpful.

Let me tell you what I just really did. As I used those words, pictures were being painted in your mind. When you hear the word *hope*, you think of an honest, optimistic, and confident expectation of things that are going to happen in the future. *Warm* is a word that's important. The word *hear* is up there too.

I have a friend out in California who woke up one morning totally, completely, irreversibly stone-deaf. That was many years ago. He said, "Zig, the thing that I miss most in life today is the fact that I can never hear my wife, my children, or my grandchildren say to me, 'I love you.'" Most of us take things like that for granted on an everyday basis.

Humor helps to build winning relationships. A person with a good sense of humor will not take themselves overly seriously. I love the story of the lady who was talking on the telephone. After a few minutes, she said, "Oh, you were trying to sell me something. Thank goodness. I thought you were trying to collect for all the stuff I've already bought."

I like the story of the door-to-door salesman who said to the prospect, "You make a down payment, and then you don't make any more payments for six months."

The guy said, "Who told you?"

A good sense of humor, I believe, comes in handy.

If we want to build winning relationships, we need to be finders of good. I love the example that Ted Engstrom uses in one of his books.

Years ago at the University of Wisconsin, there were about twenty young men who were destined for greatness. There was no question about it. They were brilliant writers. Every week, they had a little club, and they would get together, talk about, and critique what they had written.

When the group got started, it was friendly, but it gradually turned into caustic criticism. As a matter of fact, they called themselves the Stranglers.

There were also about twenty ladies who decided if those guys could get together like that, they were going to get together too. They started critiquing each other, but there was a dramatic difference: any kind of a criticism always carried a suggestion for improvement. They encouraged one another. Instead of the Stranglers, they called themselves the Wranglers.

In the end, nothing was ever heard from a single member of the Stranglers, but about five of the Wranglers, including Marjorie Kinnan Rawlings, who wrote *The Yearling*, went on to literary prominence.

When you put negative words into criticism, it does make a difference—a negative difference. We teach a program called "Born to Win." People have come from all over the world, and I mean all over the world: everybody from sixteen-year-old students to the chairman of the board of Bethlehem Steel, and everyone in between.

We encourage husbands and wives to come together. It has nothing to do with the marriage relationship per se, but hundreds of times I've seen couples arrive at each other's throats and walk out in each other's arms. They've learned to understand and appreciate each other; they've learned how to communicate and make friends with their mates.

Although I generally lecture every day in the series, most of the time is spent around a little table in groups of seven. They do a lot of participation, and every time anybody says or does anything, the other six write a note on a little pad we have called "I like because." They list some specific, observable behavior: "I like Sally because she always has a word of encouragement for me." "I like Bill because he's so friendly and outgoing." "I like Bob because he always brings his project in on time and under budget."

By the time we get through, each individual there has at least a hundred of those notes. What is the purpose of that? To teach them to start looking for the good things in the other person.

One time four couples attended the course. They were so tremendously impressed that on the first night, they went out to dinner in one of Dallas's most expensive restaurants.

They hit the jackpot with the waiter. He had been a waiter over twenty-five years. He was magnificent. He was there when he was needed, but he did not join the party. He was friendly but not familiar. If there was a need, he instantly met that need, then disappeared so that they could enjoy one another's company. He contributed enormously to the enjoyment of the meal.

When the four couples left, they left the waiter a 25 percent tip, and that's a big tip in that restaurant. Each one of them wrote him a little note: "I like you because . . ."

They walked out the front door and had gotten about a hundred feet out when all of a sudden, they heard the waiter's voice: "Wait a minute, folks. Wait a minute." He came running toward them, waving those eight slips of paper.

He drew a breath and said, "You know, I've been a waiter over twenty-five years." Then he could not continue; he started to weep. When he finally regained his composure (which they said seemed like forever, although it undoubtedly was just a few seconds), he said, "In twenty-five years of being a waiter, this is the most beautiful, the most significant thing that has ever happened to me. I will never forget tonight." With that, he turned and walked back into the restaurant.

My good friend, inspirational speaker Cavett Robert, says there are over three billion people on the face of this earth who go to bed hungry every night, but there are over four billion people who go to bed hungry every night for a word of appreciation, a word of encouragement, a compliment.

Wouldn't it be a tragedy if one of those people was your wife or your husband, your mom or your dad, your brother or your sister? Maybe it's the next-door neighbor, maybe the person you work with every day. This is a good person, a good man, a good woman, who's been there years and years, but for whatever reason, over the last few months, everything that individual touches has gone sour. One word of encouragement might mean a tremendous difference in that individual's life. Encouragement, giving hope, is one of the most powerful tools we have for building winning relationships.

Once, during a tour of Australia, I was in Melbourne. During one of the breaks, a lady came up to me and said, "Mr. Ziglar, I'm thirty-two years old. I have two little girls. They're six years old and nine years old. I've been listening to your series on raising positive kids in a negative world. Mr. Ziglar, let me tell you, my two little girls had every psychological problem known to man. They'd reverted back to infantile behavior.

"In your recording, you keep saying, 'Tell your kids that you love them. If you don't tell them that you love them, they're going to grow up getting married and have children, and then they won't tell their children they love them. Somebody has to break the chain.' Mr. Ziglar, I'm thirty-two years old. In my lifetime, I've never had a living, breathing human being say, 'I love you.'

"It was weird. It seemed that every time I put that particular tape on, it was always on that one specific spot: 'Tell your kids that you love them.'

"One night we were sitting around in the den. I was seated on the sofa. My six-year-old was at my feet, and my nine-year-old was across the room. All of a sudden I remembered, and I just blurted it out: 'Girls, I just want you to know I sure do love you.'

"My six-year-old sprang up like she'd been on a spring. She threw her arms around my neck, hugged me, kissed me, and started crying. My nine-year-old was immediately across the room. She threw her arms around me, hugged me and kissed me. By then, all three of us were crying. I don't know how long we cried. It might have only been a couple of minutes. All I know is that when we finished, we were emotionally drained, and yet there was an exhilaration that we had never experienced before.

"My little girls and I determined that night that every morning and every night for the rest of our lives when we were together, we would hug and kiss and tell each other how much we loved each other."

The woman continued, "You know, Mr. Ziglar, when I lay down that night, all of a sudden, that lifetime of bad habits and negativity started coming back in my mind. I'd never been told, 'I love you' myself, and I was wondering, was that just a blip on the screen of life? Or is there legitimate hope that something can be done?

"Then it hit me: I am their mother; I am the adult. It is my responsibility to take the action. I instinctively realized that you cannot make an overdraft on the bank of love all of your life and expect to bring the account up to date with one deposit, regardless of how big the deposit is.

"I determined that come what may, the next morning I'd grab my little girls and I'd hug them, kiss them, and tell them how much I loved them. Mr. Ziglar, I very quickly learned something: you can hug a dirty child, but it's very difficult to hug a ramrod-stiff girl. That's the way they were the next morning. To tell you the truth, I was a little stiff too, but I determined to keep it up."

The woman added, "It took us two weeks before we ever started feeling relaxed and having a natural feeling for it. In about a month, we started adding a hug when we just bumped into each other accidentally. Mr. Ziglar, in about sixty days after we got started, over 90 percent of those psychological problems had completely disappeared."

Two thousand years ago, a Jewish scholar wrote his relatives in Corinth a love letter. Some say it's the most beautiful love letter ever written. He wound it up by saying, "Love never fails" (1 Corinthians 13:8). I believe he's right. Genuine love is based on your interest in doing the right thing and the best thing for the other person.

Now please understand this. Sometimes you plant seeds that don't bring a harvest. That's part of life. Everybody that you're nice to is not necessarily going to be nice to you, but that's their problem; it's not yours. I'm convinced that over a period of time, when you persist in doing the right thing, things are going to happen.

Something tremendously exciting happens when you go out of your way to be nice to other people. The brain produces a certain chemical called serotonin. Serotonin hits the system in full force at about 10:00 in the morning. Most people start their day a little earlier than that. When you want to jump-start the flow of serotonin, do something nice for somebody else early in the morning. This activates the part of the brain that produces the chemical. You feel better about yourself. Your image improves, and as a result, you're energized. Physiologically, things do happen.

This involves change. I love what my friend, comedian Ken Davis, has to say. A young fellow was working at a restaurant or a store there, and he's ringing up sale after sale. The boss came along and said, "How's it going?"

"It's going pretty good," said the young man. I don't have trouble putting it in, and I don't have trouble getting it out. It's making the change that is the problem."

A lot of people hate to make changes. You get set in your ways, but one definition of insanity is to think you can keep on doing the same thing and somehow get different results.

You build winning relationships by creating the correct environment. For example, you get up thirty minutes earlier. That's a tremendous step toward creating the right environment in your home. Why? Because when you start your day in a dead run, run all day, and end your day in a dead run, you don't have the inclination to be as nice to people as you otherwise would. A thirty-minute start, which enables you to be a little more casual, can make a great difference.

If you're married, or if you have children, send them off with something positive, a hug and a kiss, in the morning. Later, reenter the relationship in a positive way. Many times kids come home from school griping and complaining about what happened. In most cases, they learned it from mom and dad, who, when they've been coming in from work all these years, have greeted each other with, "You can't believe what that idiot I work for did today," or, "You think that's a problem; let me tell you about mine." Then we wonder why our kids are not excited about going out, getting a job, and going to work.

Instead of doing that, make an absolute pact that when you get back together, it's going to be in a positive light. Husbands and wives, ask, "What happened to you today that's really exciting? Tell me about it. What was the best thing that happened?" When kids come in, say, "What did you learn today" or, "What happened today that was the most fun?" or, "What are you learning that I'd like to know about?" Make it positive.

I'm not advocating that you ignore any problems. I'm saying, delay serious discussion until after you've gotten back together—later that evening, after dinner, when things are settled down.

See, if kids identify coming home as negative, they're going to go join a gang. If husbands and wives identify coming back home as a negative experience, that's when they start stopping off at the bar and doing other things. Let's create an environment that makes it true and makes it good.

Let me also say this: if there is a difficulty between you and a person you love, you need to get it right as quickly as possible. You don't let it fester.

One of my favorite people is Neal Jeffrey. Neal was the quarterback for the Baylor Bears and led them to the Southwest Conference championship. Neal stutters, yet he's one of the most effective speakers I've ever heard in my life. He's never let his condition become a problem. As a matter of fact, he used that condition the most effectively I have ever seen in my life.

When Neal was young, he was very close to his dad. His dad had certain rules and regulations, as his mom did, about what time he was going to come in from dates.

One night Neal stayed a little over time, and on the way home he realized he was going to be late. He said, "Shucks, I'm already in trouble." He turned around and went back to spend a little more time with his girl, and he got home a couple of hours later than he was supposed to be.

Nobody was up and around. Neal sneaked up, and he was hoping that his dad hadn't even noticed. It was Saturday night. He got up Sunday morning and went down to breakfast, hoping that he'd get there early and his dad wouldn't be up.

There was his dad. Not a word was said. Nothing was said on Monday. Nothing was said on Tuesday. Finally, about Wednesday, Neal said he could no longer stand it. He went to his dad, and he said, "Dad, here's what I did. I was wrong. Will you forgive me?" The relationship was restored.

The more quickly you do things like that, the more easily the relationship is going to be rebuilt.

In dealing with people, including our children, I love a little example that happened to me. A family picked me up in Cleveland, Ohio: David and Jane Mezey, who have two beautiful children. Gregory was a first-grader, and Brian was a sixth-grader, who probably had the vocabulary of a tenth- or eleventh-grader.

On our way to the restaurant, Brian spoke up, saying, "Dad, if you cut left right here, you will miss some of the traffic, and we can get there sooner."

When he said that, David said, "Brian, that's a good thought. Thank you for giving it to me, but I've already calculated in my own mind that the way we're now going is a more direct route. I believe we can get there faster this way, but thank you very much for your suggestion. It was a good one."

That's what I call an authoritative response. By contrast, the authoritarian individual, whether it's in the workplace or at home, says, "You do it because I said so, that's why," or, "You do it because that's the way we've always done it." The authoritative person, which is what David was, simply says, "We're going to do it this way, and let me explain why."

David was courteous to his son: he showed him respect. He gave him a logical explanation, simply saying, "I've already thought this one through, and here's why this one would be better," but he also thanked him. I don't need to tell you they have a tremendous relationship between the two of them.

The relationships between husbands and wives are, of course, the most important ones. Journalist Sydney Harris says, "The only way to understand a woman is to love her. Then it isn't necessary to understand her." We fellows laugh about this a whole lot. They say, "Women understand women; they don't like each other. We don't understand them; we just love them." I know that's the way I feel about the redhead.

The best way to build a lifetime relationship is to make your mate your best friend. There are some things you'd never say or do to your best friend. Make your mate your best friend, and the relationship will be much better.

Isn't it ironic? The communications technology that we have today is so enormously effective, yet communication individually, one-on-one, is a bigger problem today than it has ever been. Similarly, in primitive societies, they don't have any timepieces, but they have lots of time. In our society, we have incredible numbers of timepieces, but somehow or another, we don't have any time.

In the April 1993 issue of *The Atlantic Monthly*, there is an article about the importance of the family. It points out that in single-parent families, children are six times as likely to be poor. They're two to three times as likely to have behavioral and emotional problems. They're far more likely to quit school, become pregnant, abuse drugs, and get in trouble with the law.

Furthermore, 70 percent of the juveniles in state reform facilities are from fatherless homes. The chances of being physically or sexually abused in these homes are forty times as great as they are in the two-parent family. That doesn't necessarily mean that the stepparent is the abuser, but a lot of times with the natural father and mother, there's a respect shown that otherwise is not.

Let me stress, however, that I never say anything with the purpose of hanging a guilt trip on anybody. As I frequently say, 99 percent of the people do what they do when they do it based on the information they have at that time and the circumstances that existed at that time. As a matter of fact, I was raised by a single mother. My wife was raised by a single mother. They were both widowed when we were very small.

SIX

You Never Know How Far It Goes

Several years go, at the cafeteria at Southwestern Seminary in Fort Worth, they had a sign at the beginning of the serving line in front of the apples that said, "God is watching. Take only one."

As you went down the line and got to the end of it, they had the cookies. The sign there said, "Take as many as you want. God is busy watching the apples."

Then there was the time when the pope was making his tour of America. A lot of people don't know this, but he loves to drive cars. He had never driven a fancy limousine, and obviously they had the very best for him. He'd been all over the place, being chauffeured around. It came time for him to go back to the airport to catch the plane, and he told the chauffeur, he said, "You know, I've never driven one of these. Let me drive."

The chauffeur tried to talk the pope out of it, but he said, "No, I'm an excellent driver, and I want to drive." He was an excellent driver, but he did drive a little fast. He got out on the freeway and had that sucker really going. He heard the siren behind him and saw the flashing lights.

The pope pulled over to the side. The patrolman got out, walked up, took one look at the pope, and said, "Excuse me." He went back to his patrol car, called headquarters, and said, "Hey, we have serious problem."

"What's the problem?"

"We have a big one."

"Well, is it the mayor?"

"Oh, no. He's bigger than that."

"Is it the governor?"

"Oh, no. He's lots bigger than that."

"Well, how big is he?"

"I don't know, but he has to be a big one. He has the pope as his chauffeur."

There are many important people in life, but let's explore the philosophy of how you can have everything in life you want if you'll help enough other people get what they want.

How does it work in the corporate world? Let me give you some data. Between 1974 and 1991, American exports of automobiles to Japan declined 2 percent. During the same period, German exports of automobiles to Japan increased over 700 percent.

Why did the Germans get so many more cars into Japan? At one point they sent an entourage from Berlin to Tokyo. The entourage landed, caught a cab down to the hotel where they'd be staying, looked around for a day or two, and then caught a plane back to Berlin.

"We've made an astonishing discovery," they said. "The Japanese drive smaller cars than we do, and would you believe they put the steering wheels on the right-hand side of the automobile? It's because they drive on the left side of the road. Maybe if we build smaller cars and put the steering wheel on the right, the Japanese would buy our cars."

The Germans built the cars that way, and sure enough, that's exactly what happened. The Japanese said, "Hey, we like these automobiles. Send them on over here."

At one point around the same time, there was a showroom displaying the new Jeep that Chrysler was selling over there, and Japanese were excited about it. The crowds were gathering around it, and they were buying that car like crazy. They could not keep them in stock. Why the difference all of a sudden?

Chrysler did a very smart thing. You may have already guessed what it was. They put the steering wheel on the right-hand side of the automobile.

What did the Japanese want? Cars with steering wheels on the right-hand side. What did the Germans want? They wanted to sell cars. The Germans helped the Japanese get what they want, so they got what they wanted. It's not that complicated.

Again, you can have everything in life you want if you'll just help enough other people get what they want.

It really does begin with us. I had the privilege of being on a program with John Mackovic, who at the time was head football coach at the University of Texas. He made this observation: "When we have the ball, I'm very much interested in the defense the other team has, but I know deep down if I've recruited the right athletes, if I have trained them and taught them as they need to be taught, if I've developed the right plan of action, regardless of the defense they throw at me, I'm going to get my share of points." In other words, he's saying, "The action really does start here, with me."

How did Chrysler sell Jeeps? Very simple. They took the initiative. I wonder how many Japanese cars would be in America today if they had insisted on putting the steering wheel on the right-hand side.

In other words, we have to look at the other person and find out what they want in the relationship. It's not what you *think* they want, but it's the way they want to be treated.

Let me refer you to the December 8, 1989 issue of *The Wall Street Journal.* It talks about the Golden Rule companies: they act according to the principle do unto others as you want them to do unto you.

They discovered something rather intriguing about these companies. Number one, they grow faster. Number two, they make more money. Number three, they have a greater return on equity than do the other companies.

What kind of doctor, what kind of store, what kind of service person do you want to go with? Isn't it always somebody who has a prime interest in you, who's absolutely honest, whose integrity is beyond question, whom you can absolutely trust?

The reality is, these companies are more profitable. In the December 1989 issue of *Executive Excellence*, there's an article by Ken Blanchard, author of *The One Minute Manager*. In it he points out that had you invested $30,000 in the stock market across the board thirty years before, you would have had roughly $109,000. Had you taken the same $30,000 and invested it in the fifteen companies that have integrity as the base from which they operate and a stated policy that they're in business to serve the public, you'd have over $1 million.

With integrity, as I've often said, you have nothing to fear, because you have nothing to hide. Let's see if we can tie all of this, again, into the way we deal with other people.

Many years ago, just outside of Boston, there was a mental institution, which for its day was well advanced. Nevertheless, it had a dungeon downstairs, where they put the ones for whom there was no hope.

They had a little girl named Little Annie. She had tremendous mood swings. One day she was kind and loving and gentle, and on other days she became almost a little animal. She was impossible to predict, so they had her down in the dungeon.

There was a nurse in that institution who was nearing the age of retirement. For whatever reason, she started going down there every day and having her lunch just outside of the cage where Little Annie was being housed. She wouldn't necessarily talk to her. She might speak, might say a few things, but she was there every day, in her own way communicating to her, "You are a human being. I do love you. I have an interest in you."

One day the nurse took some brownies and put them inside. Little Annie ignored them, but the next day the nurse noticed that the brownies were gone. The next Thursday, she took some more brownies down, and the process continued.

The doctors noticed that there was improvement in Little Annie. They decided they would move her up and put her into the treatment process. Later they pronounced her well. They said, "You can leave now. You're OK. You can function in society."

Little Annie said, "No. This has meant so much to me. It has given my life back. I would like to stick around for at least a few years and pay back by doing some things for some other people."

Many years later, when Helen Keller received England's highest recognition for a foreigner, Queen

Victoria asked her to whom she attributed her remarkable success in life, despite all of her handicaps. Without any hesitation, Helen Keller said, "Had it not been for Anne Sullivan, this would not have happened." That woman was Little Annie. In relationship building, you never know how far it's going to go.

When I was a teenager, I wanted to get in the Naval Air Corps. It was my dream. World War II was going on. I wanted to fly those airplanes shooting down the enemy, come home a conquering hero, and have a ticker-tape parade in Yazoo City, Mississippi.

I knew that I had a basic problem. Number one, my grades in school had not been the best. As a matter of fact, I was in that part of the class that made the upper half possible, if you know what I mean. But between my junior and senior year, I decided to go to summer school and pick up some extra math and science so I would be better prepared to get into the Naval Air Corps.

I had to take a course in American history in order to get my high-school diploma, and it griped me no end. "Why should I take this course in history? What good is it going to do me to know what happened one or two hundred years ago? I want to take some math and science so I can learn how to fly those airplanes, shoot down enemies, win the war, and come back a hero."

I had no choice. They said, "You have to take the class in order to graduate. No high-school graduation certificate, no Naval Air Corps."

I walked into history class that first day with a chip on my shoulder. I sat and thought, "I'm going to get enough out of this to pass, and that'll be the end of anything I have to do with history."

Coach Joby Harris was the teacher, and he threw me a curve. He turned salesman that day, and what a magnificent sales job he did. He sold us on why I had to know my history. I walked out of there that day a history major, and it was the only course I consistently made A's in for the rest of my academic career.

Today my favorite subject is history. The best book I've read in the last twenty-five years is a history book: *The Light and the Glory: 1492-1793 (God's Plan for America)*, by Peter Marshall and David Manuel. It reads like a novel. It gives you the real story of America—what really happened—and it's extremely well documented and researched.

Coach Harris did something else that day. He turned out to be a prophet, way ahead of his time. It was 1943. He said, "Those of you who have an ability that goes beyond just providing for your own needs have a responsibility and an opportunity to reach down and lift up those people who do not have that same ability and opportunity. As a matter of fact, if we don't reach down and help others up, the day is going to come when by sheer weight of numbers, they're going to reach up and pull us down."

That's exactly what is happening and has already happened—in terms of standard of living, educational levels, the whole schmear. Our "I Can" course, which is taught in many schools, is the direct result of that. The financial cost on our part has been substantial, yet I believe it's one of the most important things we have ever done. Youngsters today tell me, "Fifteen or ten years ago, I took the course. Let me tell you what happened."

The work I've been doing in the drug war and the prisons and churches and other places is a direct result of what Coach Joby Harris said to me in history class. You can affect people, and you never know how many people that you are going to affect.

When Coach Joby Harris was a youngster, he was a Boy Scout. His Scoutmaster, who also was the first Scoutmaster and Scout official in the state of Mississippi, was a gentleman named Thomas B. Abernathy. Mr. Abernathy, for whatever reason, took an unusual interest in Joby Harris. Although Joby had a father, Mr. Abernathy became a second father, a mentor, to him. He taught him all about scouting, but he also taught him a lot of other things.

Mr. Abernathy had four children: three daughters and a son. His youngest daughter is a girl named Jean, and Jean Abernathy has been Mrs. Zig Ziglar since 1946. There's no way on earth Mr. Abernathy could ever have known that when he was spending the time influencing Joby Harris, he was teaching the man who would have such an impact on his future son-in-law, the father of his yet unborn grandchildren. You never know what's going to happen when you do something for somebody, but the story is not over.

World War II was winding down. They decided not to continue the flight training, so I never even got to it. I was still in the college portion when the war ended. I never got into the Naval Air Corps, but if your son or daughter were to go to Corpus Christi, Texas, today and become a naval aviator, they would take our business development course, "See You at the Top." All instructors are required to take it before they can train young pilots.

We never know. The influence you have today, the good you do today, is going to live and live and keep on living. Your attitude affects your relationships with your people, and it also affects their income. The way you see them determines how you treat them. The way you treat them has a direct bearing on their performance.

Let me give you another personal example of what I'm talking about. At age twenty-five, after I finally got my start in selling, I became the youngest divisional supervisor in the sixty-six-year history of that company. We were in cookware sales, and in direct sales the field managers are the ones who really control the organization's destiny. Their daily contact with the salespeople, their training, their inspiration, their leadership, their problem solving, and their guidance and direction are enormously important.

When I was promoted to the position of divisional supervisor, I had in turn to promote a person who was really not ready or qualified to move to the field manager level, but I had no other options, so it just had to be.

When I got the promotion, that division was going really gung-ho, but almost immediately things started to happen. The manager who had taken my place did not have the experience, so that organization collapsed. Another field manager had a heart attack, which took him out of operation, and his part of the organization collapsed too.

Still another man had his big toe almost completely cut off. He spent twenty days in the hospital, and for the next four months he was on crutches. He was largely negated in terms of doing the necessary field work. His organization went kaput. Yet another manager had an integrity problem—which always brings difficulty—and his part of the organization caved in as well.

Here's the scene. One month we have a gung-ho, going, moving organization, and two months later, it's still going, but all of it is downhill. A rumor got started that the company was going to replace me: I could not handle it, I didn't have enough experience, I was too young.

Now you're talking about somebody who had a pity party. Old Zig really had one: "I'm the good guy. I didn't have anything to do with that heart attack. I didn't have anything to do with cutting that toe off. I didn't have anything to do with the fact that I had no choice to promote someone who wasn't qualified. I had nothing to do with that integrity problem. It's not my fault."

I really felt put upon: "I'm the good guy, and they're saying those ugly things about me. That ain't right." I had an advanced case of stinking thinking. It was fast settling into hardening of the attitude. I desperately needed a checkup from the neck up.

At the time we were living in Knoxville, Tennessee. I walked down Main Street there and saw a new book in the shop window. Its title was *The Power of Positive Thinking*. I said, "Boy, if anybody has ever needed some positive thinking, it's Old Zig."

I walked in, I picked that sucker up, and I started reading it walking out the front door. I was on my way to the airport to catch a flight down to Nashville, where I'd been scheduled for several months to speak to another division of the company on—guess what?—positive thinking. Here was the guy with the worst attitude in the division being invited to speak on positive thinking.

I got into that book, and I realized that the author, Dr. Norman Vincent Peale, had written it specifically for me. He kept saying, "Now, Zig, I agree with you. You are not responsible for the heart attack. You're right, Zig. You had nothing to do with the big toe. You're absolutely right, Zig. You had nothing to do with all of those things, but let me tell you what you are responsible for. You're responsible for the way you handle that situation. It's not what happens to you. It's how you handle what happens to you that makes the difference."

Let's have a quick reality check. Some people are so "positive" that they lose their judgment. They think it's negative to ever say, "Here's a problem." That is not being negative. Identifying a problem is not being negative. But it is negative when you say, "Here's a problem, and there's nothing I can do about it. It's unsolvable." That's negative. Positive thinking identifies the problem and says, "Let me see how I am going to solve it."

Before I got a third of the way through Dr. Peale's book, I started looking at each one of the divisions and saying, "Now here's something we can do, and here's something we can do, and here's something we can do"—a dramatic, total, 100 percent turn-around.

Let me emphasize that the economy had not changed. The toe was still in bad shape, the heart was still in bad shape, the integrity was getting in a little better shape, and experience was being gained on the other end. Within sixty more days, we were doing more business than we had been doing when all of those things happened. What changed? The thinking of the person in charge.

One of my favorite statements when I do leadership conferences is, "When you have one stinking thinking, inept worker, you have one stinking thinking, inept worker, but when you have one stinking thinking leader, you have an organization full of inept producers."

I'd been promoted in May. We finished that year twenty-second out of sixty-six divisions. The next year we were fifth. The next year we were third: New York and Kansas were the only two states that beat us. What happened?

What happened was very simple. Instead of having a pity party, my attitude changed. I started analyzing all of the strong qualities and the good things that these managers could be doing, and the results were absolutely dramatic. I got so excited about it.

Let me simply say that I had a big promotion followed by a big collapse. I caught the PLOM disease, "poor little old me" disease, big time. I spread the stinking thinking, and the solution was, I read a book.

Yes, you really can have everything in life you want if you will just help enough other people get what they want. I will say that enough times that I can guarantee you it's going to become a tremendous part of your life.

Some years ago I had the privilege of going back to Hinds Junior College, which is now known as Hinds Community College, in Raymond, Mississippi, to help set up a scholarship fund for Coach Joby Harris and his wife, Jim El. It was an exciting occasion. I spoke to the student body, the faculty, and some visitors that morning, and that afternoon, we had a public seminar in Jackson.

The meeting on campus was truly exciting to me, and out of it I got a tremendous lesson. The auditorium was packed, and I looked at the students and faculty lined up all the way around the auditorium. As I started, I said, "Now, folks, if you will notice, we have five vacant seats down here, and four vacant seats over here. All you have to do is come down and claim them. They are yours." Only one person moved.

Then I said, "There are no obstacles. I wish I was strong enough and had the time to pick them up and take them back to you. First of all, I'm not, second of all, I don't have time, and third, I'm sure the administration would be very unhappy if I could pull a Superman and do exactly that. Come on down. They're available." Still, only the one came down. None came to the second row.

"Now," I said, "I'll be the first to confess you're going to have to climb over two people to get to these four seats, but that's the way life is. Sometimes you have to climb over obstacles in order to get there, but I can tell you it's well worth it. The front row seats are available."

There's a lot of room at the top. There's just not enough room to sit down. You know what the difficult part is? It's getting out of the crowd at the bottom. That's the tough part, because at the bottom you have tens of thousands of people. It takes a whole lot for you to be able to stick your head high enough even to be seen, but once you take that first step out of the crowd at the bottom, the competition starts to diminish dramatically.

A number of years ago, I ran an ad in a newspaper in Houston. At the same time, I ran an ad in Denver. I'll not identify what the response was from which city, but in one of the ads, I'd said, "Earn $20,000 a year." In the other ad, it said, "Earn $50,000 a year." I got twenty-five times as many responses to the one on the lower figure, because most people at that time could not see themselves earning the higher dollars.

Most people never really see themselves as the capable individuals they are. That's the reason I spend so much time on building a healthy self-image. I just want you to know that front row seats are available, but they're not going to come to you. There are obstacles to climb, but they really are climbable.

How do you climb obstacles? I love the picture of the person standing at the foot of a flight of stairs. Over there is an elevator, and the sign above it says, "The elevator to the top is out of order. You're going to have to take the stairs."

I believe that's the way it is in life. The elevator to the top is out of order, and yes, you are going to have to take the stairs in order to get there. I believe, ladies and gentlemen, that winning relationships and friends are going to be playing an important part.

I love the story of the little guy that was trying to get his dad's attention. His dad was ignoring him; he was busy with other things. The little boy got very insistent. He said, "Dad, who's your favorite? Do you like Superman or Batman better?"

The father said, "Oh, son, I'm busy."

"But, Daddy, just tell me. Which one do you like the best, Superman or Batman?"

Finally the father said, "OK, Superman is my favorite."

The little boy said, "Well, Daddy, Batman is my favorite."

The father said, "That's nice, son, but Superman is mine."

Then the little boy said, "But, Daddy, aren't you going to ask me why Batman is my favorite?"

"OK, Son. Why is Batman your favorite?"

The little boy looked at him and said, "Daddy, Batman has a friend."

The father finally got the point. He said, "That's important to you, isn't it, son?"

"Yes, Daddy, it is."

Aren't we all looking for friends? Don't we all need that attention? Isn't it true particularly within our families? Isn't it true that the applause of a single human being is of great consequence? Doesn't it affect our productivity, our happiness, and everything we do in every area of our life? It really boils down to becoming interested in the other person. It really does.

There's no such thing, folks, as somebody who does not have value. Everyone has value. When we recognize and encourage that value, it's amazing what can happen as a result.

*   *   *

I want to close by telling you a love story. It's a little different from most love stories, but it really does have a lot to say. It's a love story about the game of golf.

Nothing pleases me any more than to get out there on the hillside or on the golf course, and I like to tee that sucker up so I can get at it. I rear back, and when I do, I let the string all the way out. I hit that sucker as far as I can. Boom. Then, if I can find it, I hit that sucker again.

I found out a long time ago that a slow game of golf and a fast game of golf in reality both take about the same amount of time. It'll take you about five hours, counting getting there, getting ready, and warming up, to play it and get back home.

I travel a lot, and I wasn't about to come home, kiss the redhead and my son good-bye, and head for the golf course, but I love to play golf. So I did something really bright, if I do say so myself. I bought my wife and my son a set of golf clubs. Everybody was excited about it, except my wife and son.

They went along with me for about five games. At the end of about the fifth game, the redhead said, "Honey, I just do not like to play golf. It's too hot, or it's too cold. It's too wet, or it's too windy. You're just going to have to count me out." There went golf buddy number one.

At the end of the summer, my boy said, "Dad, I hardly know how to tell you this. I know how much you like to play golf. Dad, I like to be with you, and I know you like to be with me, but golf is just not my game, Dad. I'll wrestle with you, I'll throw the football with you, I'll go fishing with you, I'll ride bikes with you, but, Dad, golf is just not my game. Count me out." There went golf buddy number two.

For the next three years, there wasn't much golf in my life. One night I was back in town, and we'd been out to dinner. We were on Dallas's North Central Expressway, and we passed a driving range. All of a sudden my boy spoke up. He said, "Dad, let's stop and hit a few golf balls."

My son is a smooth talker. So we stopped to hit a few golf balls. We were banging away, and suddenly he said, "Dad, let me borrow one of your woods." So I pulled my four wood out of the bag and handed it to him.

My boy choked up on it a little bit, reared back, and he cold-cocked that sucker about forty yards further than he had ever hit a golf ball before in his life. When he turned around, that smile on his face clearly said, "Ziglar, you've got yourself a golfing buddy now." It was the second most beautiful smile I've ever seen on his face.

The most beautiful one was a few days later. We were out at the club playing. We were out on the par fours. My boy took that four wood, and again he let the string out. He busted that sucker right down the middle. It had a little draw on it, hit the ground running like a scared rabbit, and stopped dead center, right in the middle of the fairway—a perfect position.

We got to that ball. He took the five iron out, and just as you see them doing on television, he kept his head down. He smooth-stroked it. It took off, got right over the green, and landed just as soft as a feather about forty feet from the cup. He was hunting his bird. (If you're not a golfer, that simply means that if he sinks that putt, he's one under par on that hole. If you don't know what that means, it means he done good.)

I showed my boy how to line the putt. I showed him how to stroke it, and when he stroked it, there was zero doubt about it. It was in the cup all the way. When that ball hit the bottom of that cup, that boy jumped about six feet straight up in the air, still beating me to ground by five seconds. Man alive, was there ever excitement.

I grabbed him and hugged him, and we did a little dance for a couple of minutes. Then it occurred to me that I had a problem. I was on the green in two also. I was hunting my bird too. I was only about ten feet from the cup. I knew that if I missed the putt, my son would figure I'd missed it on purpose so he could win. That would have given him a cheap victory, which is quite a loss.

So I determined I was going to do the very best I could, so that if I did miss it, I could honestly say, "Congratulations, son. You won it fair and square."

I lined the putt as well as I know how to line a putt. I stroked it as well as I've ever stroked a putt in my life, and just as if it had eyes, it went straight to the bottom of the cup. Before I reached down to pick it up, I looked at my boy, and I said, "Now, tell me the truth, son. Were you pulling for Dad?"

He was eleven years old. He'd never beaten his dad at a hole of golf. It would have meant an awful lot to him at that point. If I had missed, he would have won the hole. Without any hesitation, quietly but very firmly, he looked me right in the eye and said, "Dad, I always pull for you."

That, ladies and gentlemen, is love. That's pure love.

That's what we need more of in Dallas and Portland and San Diego and Albany. It's what we need more of in every home in every county in every state in this great land of ours. We need it between the parent and the child, between the husband and the wife, between the employer and the employee, between the teacher and the student.

We need somebody who is pulling for us to do our very best, because there's an old saying that people don't really care how much you know until they know how much you care about them.

When you really are pulling for the other person, there is a persuasiveness that becomes part of you that is beyond belief. When you're pulling for your child to do something for their benefit, when you're pulling for a customer to buy because deep down you know it's for their benefit, when you're pulling for an employee to perform better because it is to their benefit, when you're pulling for anybody to do something because they're going to be the winner, you become instantly more effective, instantly more professional, instantly more persuasive. Love is a tremendous persuader.

Every year in Yazoo City, we have family reunions. Because we live in Dallas, the other members of family live much closer. We generally fly to Jackson, rent a car, and stop by the grocery store to buy our contribution to the big spread. The other members of the family bring theirs in already cooked.

Several years ago, we stopped by to get the things we were going to buy: a smoked ham and a smoked turkey, some little snacks, and a number of canned soft drinks. We got to the checkout stand, and the cashier figured it up. The redhead had her checkbook out. She wrote the check, and as she handed the check to the cashier, she automatically reached into her wallet to pull out her driver's license and several credit cards.

As she did so, she said, "You probably will want to see these." The cashier never looked down. She was looking at the check. As she did, she said, "No. In Yazoo City, the name Ziglar is all the identification we need."

I left that city in 1943. The cashier didn't recognize me or my name. She was talking about my mother and older brothers and older sisters, who had left us a legacy that is beyond price. Legacies are left through relationships—the way you deal with people. It's the basic foundation upon which you have built.

When we build that right foundation, when our heart is right, when we really do have an interest in others, when we live with integrity, then we can live and leave something that will last infinitely longer than we will live.

I think Dr. Jack Graham sums it up as well as anybody when he said, "Wealth is the total of what you have that money can't buy and death can't take away."

I believe with all of my heart that if you buy the ideas and concepts I've been talking about in this book, I'll be able to close this by saying, as I always do, "I'll see you, and yes, I really do mean you, at the top."

God bless you.